LETTERING

FOR

ADVERTISING

LETTERING

FOR

ADVERTISING

mortimer leach

 Reinhold Publishing Corporation • New York

iv

CONTENTS

To Betty, Nancy and Laurie

ACKNOWLEDGMENTS

This book covers the basic data necessary for the understanding and execution of various letterforms. It is intended, once these basic forms have been mastered, that they serve as a point of departure from which the designer may experiment with more sophisticated expressions of lettering.

I wish to express my thanks to Harvey Thompson who made the layouts for this book; to James Real, Albert Dorne, and Bill Tara, for their advice and encouragement, and to my assistants, Olavi Aho and Doyald Young, for their considerable help in the preparation of this book.

My thanks, also, to the artists and advertising agencies for their cooperation in supplying examples of professional lettering.

PREFACE

I am happy to contribute a preface to this book and to say a few words about Mort Leach. I've known and worked with him for nearly ten years now, and in my opinion, he is one of the finest and most dedicated craftsmen I have ever met.

As one of the country's top lettering men, Mort exhibits unending interest and enthusiasm; and he knows his craft. He can, and will, trace its origins and development for you back through the tradition of pure forms derived from the early Roman influences. But he is equally fascinated with the problem of giving clarity, beauty and function to the name on next year's automobile, whether it be pressed in the hub cap or embossed on the instrument panel.

I believe all crafts have one thing in common—the really great practitioners have something special and indefinable that set them apart from the rest of us. Whatever this intangible quality is, Mort has it. Somehow, he manages to impart the utmost meaning and vitality to a word or a line of lettering.

He was given the task of evolving alphabets for Chevrolet newspaper advertisements to be used for captions and subcaptions in Roman and Italic, bold, light and condensed. We wanted a face that would fit with Century body type, but it had to have a character that would extend through all the newspaper schedule and lend a personality so that, typographically speaking, all the ads would relate visually to establish penetration and memorability. His contribution proved to be so effective that his alphabet was used not only in newspapers but in magazines as well.

I don't know what better endorsement I could give Mort as the author of this book. In an age of mechanization, he's a modern craftsman in the best sense of that old word—a man with a message that warrants our attention.

James N. Hastings
VICE-PRESIDENT AND ART DIRECTOR
CAMPBELL-EWALD COMPANY, DETROIT

LETTERING
FOR
ADVERTISING

FOREWORD

There will always be a demand for good lettering artists in the commercial art field.

Our present day advertisements are planned by a group of specialists within an advertising agency and produced for the agency by specialists in the graphic arts field. Many people contribute their individual talents and skills to the building of an advertisement. Among these specialists is the lettering artist.

To the general public, lettering is one of the lesser-known arts. Very few are aware of the fact that the majority of advertising captions are hand-lettered. Most attempts at explaining the business of lettering for reproduction are usually met with the remark, "Why, I thought they just printed that!" I remember describing my work to an interested lady, some years ago. When I said that the letters were not just type, but were lettered by hand, she asked in amazement, "Do you mean to say that you letter the headline in *every* magazine?" Sounds incredible, but it's true.

Fortunately, the advertising business recognizes the value of good lettering and its contribution to a complete advertisement. It is a proven fact that a well-lettered caption serves in drawing the reader's eye to the advertiser's message and, after all, that's what he's spending his money for! Because the lettering artist can bypass the restrictions imposed by the use of type, the caption can be made to conform to the general pattern and mood of the layout, without compromises. Many captions are designed in an arrangement that would be impossible to achieve with the use of type.

Package designing offers an excellent opportunity to the artist who can letter. Surveys show that an attractively lettered container or label helps to move the product at point-of-sale.

Although lettering is an ancient art, the use of lettering specialists in the advertising field is a comparatively recent development. In the last 25 or 30 years this specialty has gained in importance and has assumed its rightful place in the advertising art structure. The lettering artist is depended upon to produce a caption to fill the requirements of any advertisement, but he often is the one who leads the way to new styles by experimentation, and in his personal interpretation of standard letter forms.

However, the knowledge of lettering should not be confined to specialists alone. The art director or designer with a sufficient lettering background can indicate his captions with assurance and speed. If his indications show the style and weight he plans for the finished art, in readable and workable form, the lettering specialist he employs will be more likely to turn in a job that satisfies his requirements. As a matter of fact, these art directors, by their interesting arrangements and objective use of lettering styles, are a source of inspiration to the lettering man. I've talked to many lettering artists about this, and they all agree that it's far easier to turn out a better job for the art director who knows lettering and can clearly indicate his ideas on the layout.

Naturally then, I feel that all art students who plan to enter the field as advertising layout men, or similar forms of the graphic arts, should spend a sufficient amount of time learning to letter. The beginner must learn to draw the basic alphabets which had an influence on the design of most type and lettered forms in use today. Only after he has accomplished this, can he safely attempt to render the more sophisticated and objective renderings with logic, and in good taste. There are still too many captions appearing in advertisements today lettered by men who try to "create" without a sufficient knowledge of the classic forms. Some of these captions are rather frightening.

To know the basic forms well, the student should familiarize himself with the history of letters and the effect of tools upon their development. Only when he learns *why* individual letters are so formed, will he avoid being a mere copyist of the work of other lettering men. Although one could begin with a study of the original Roman Capitals, the student will develop a richer background if he travels more deeply into history. An excellent source will be found in the interesting and informative books which include the history of letters, written by Tommy Thompson and Oscar Ogg.

After many years of teaching at Art Center School, Los Angeles, I have accumulated records of the most common mistakes and misinterpretations made by the average beginner. This experience has been extremely helpful to me in presenting an analysis of letter forms; it is my hope that it will be equally valuable to the reader in helping him to avoid these mistakes from the beginning.

I have found that many students approach lettering classes feeling that it's merely a routine "must" in their general studies, and happily discover that it can be a pleasurable and fascinating form of expression. After more than twenty years in the business, I still find it so.

Los Angeles

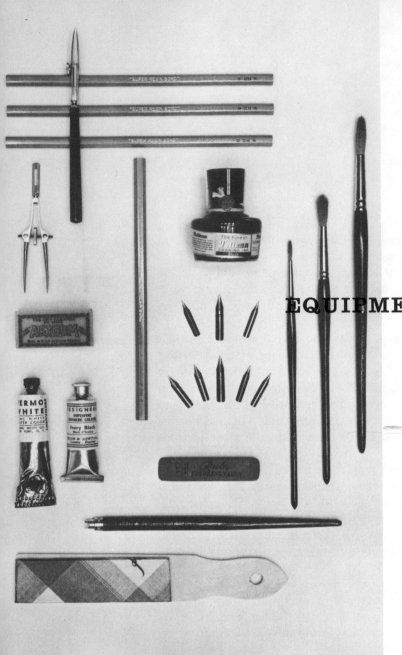

Drawing table or board
Metal edge for drawing board
Steel T-square
Triangles
Set of mechanical drawing instruments
Ruler

EQUIPMENT AND TOOLS

Pencils   Lampblack
Pencil holder   Sandpaper block
Brushes   Art gum
Penholders   Pink pearl eraser
Pen points   Sand eraser
India ink   Masking tape
Extra-dense India ink   Layout pad
White paint   Bond pad

Strathmore drawing paper 3-ply
Marsh drawing board 3-ply
White boxboard for drawing board cover

The artist's or student's choice of a particular make of drawing equipment is a personal one. A tool that will produce good results for one person may not satisfy another. The choice of pens, brushes, paints, paper, etc., calls for experiment by the beginner until he finds what is best for him. Experienced artists usually try out new products as they appear on the market with the hope of making their work easier (it's never really easy!) and occasionally find a tool or paper that is an improvement on the make they've been using.

When specific trade names have been mentioned, I've done so because these products have worked well for me and other lettering artists with whom I've checked. I recommend that they be tried along with other brands.

Most drawing pencils on the market today are standard in quality, so the choice is yours.

It is best to keep an adequate supply of pencils handy. Don't make the work more difficult by using a short stub. The use of pencil holders will save you money, but many of those available today will not fit all makes of pencils. I recommend the use of General and Hardmuth flat sketching pencils for stroke-out exercises taken up later in the book.

Penholders for lettering should be slim, with a ferrule not much larger than the thickness of a drawing pencil. A thick penholder is not easily controlled. When drawing small letters, the artist's sensitivity to the touch of the pen point on the paper is lessened if he works with a bulky penholder.

The Gillott pen points (#291, 290, 170, and 303) are most generally used by lettering artists and I recommend them as a first choice, although the equivalent sizes in Hunt and Esta-brook pen points may be preferred. The most commonly used Gillott pen points are the 290 for small or refined letters and the 170 for letters of average size and weight. The 291, which is more flexible than the 290, works well for tiny letters and is useful in the approach to loose, free-style scripts, as the easy spread of the points under pressure produces a considerable varia-tion between the thin and thick strokes. This highly sensitive pen should be used only on hard-surface papers because it may snag and spatter ink on toothy stock.

The 303 is a rigid pen with a slightly thinner point than the 170. It works well on toothy paper because its rigidity keeps it from picking up the paper surface.

Do not allow dried ink to collect on a pen point. If this should happen, soak the point in a solution of ammonia and wipe it carefully before using it again.

Winsor-Newton brushes (series 7) have long been the favorites of most lettering artists, and I recommend their use, with Grumbacher brushes as an alternate choice. It is best to use a #1 or #2 brush for retouching letters with white paint and lampblack. Beginners often think that the smallest sizes (0 and 00) should be used because of their finer tips, but these sizes do not hold enough paint and tend to dry too quickly. I suggest that you keep a separate brush for white and one for lampblack. If they are used for color, it calls for frequent washing out with soap, which tends to shorten a brush's life.

For drawing Brush Scripts or Brush Letters, the choice may range from #1 to #6. All brushes used for color should be washed with pure white soap and cold water when the work is completed. Be sure that all the color is out before putting the brush away. If you treat your pens and brushes well, they will give you long and loyal service.

There are several good makes of India ink available. Higgins, Pelican, and Artone are dependable brands. Extra-dense inks can be used for filling in large letters.

Tracing tissues used for lettering preparation should be sufficiently transparent to allow one to see his previous run-through clearly. Heavy, oily tracing tissue should be avoided. The oily surface will cause smudging and make erasures difficult.

Mechanical drawing instruments should be bought with care. It's false economy to buy a cheap set. I have seen students ruin a meticulous trace-down by using a faulty ruling pen, or an undependable pair of dividers. A good set of instruments can last through one's professional life (barring light-fingered fellow workers) and give fine service. Dietzgen, and Keuffel and Esser instruments are among the best. It's sad, but true, that, up till now, most European makes are superior to our American instruments.

Strathmore kid-finish 3-ply drawing paper will meet the requirements for most lettering assignments. It has enough tooth to keep the pen stroke under control and will take colors well. Strathmore plate finish, because of its hard, slick surface is a good paper to use for small or delicate letters, but the beginner may find it a bit too slippery, before he has gained complete control of his pen. Marsh board offers a compromise between these two. It has a minute tooth which keeps the pen from skidding and yet will accept a fine hairline stroke.

Among the several makes of white paint, Permo White is popular for retouching letters, but here again, one should experiment with other brands. The paint should be smoothly ground to allow the brush to come to a fine point and yet cover one's mistakes with a minimum of strokes. I also recommend Winsor-Newton lampblack for the final retouching.

The most comfortable working position is over a tilted drawing table, or drawing board. Although most drawing boards are cut reasonably square, the use of a metal edge on the drawing board and a steel T-square insures accuracy for the professional.

ABCDE

CONSULT OUR AUTHORIZED TRAVEL AGENTS OR

United States Lines

Nutritionists say:

"Tremendously important for everyone!"–

Hunt...for the best

BASIC RULES FOR LETTERING

These are the first rules that must be followed by the beginner before he can expect to letter captions of even tone and balance. They apply to alphabets which contain thick and thin strokes.

All the weights of the letters in a caption must appear to be the same weight optically.

On medium or light-face letters, the weighted vertical and diagonal strokes will appear optically related if they are the same width. However, on bold-face letters, the diagonal lines must be reduced a fraction to be optically even in weight to the vertical lines. (Fig. 1).

Fig. 1

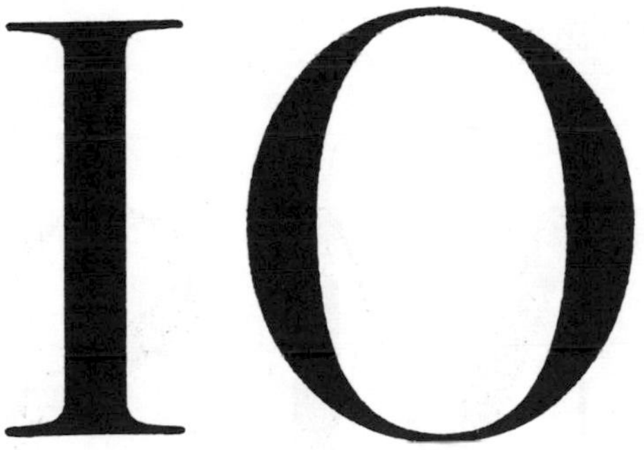

The weight of the curved strokes, at their widest point, must be drawn wider than the width of the vertical strokes, to make them appear optically alike in weight. Once a curved stroke reaches its greatest width, the weight diminishes as it departs from that point. If the width of the curve, at its widest point, is drawn exactly the same width as the vertical stems, the curved letter will appear to be lighter in weight. (Fig. 2).

Fig. 2

Top O is drawn heavier at its widest point than width of vertical I. Bottom O is same width as the vertical stems and appears lighter.

7

All the thin lines must be alike in weight. Any discrepancy in the weights of the hairlines will disrupt the even tone of a line more obviously than a variation in the heavy lines. In some alphabets, the hairlines tend to widen as they travel toward a curve or serif, but at their thinnest point they must be equal in weight. The strict observance of this rule is especially important in the execution of alphabets which contain hairlines of constant weight such as Bodoni and Didot. (Fig. 3).

Fig. 3

The curves at the top or bottom of a letter must be drawn a fraction above and/or below the horizontal guidelines. Once these curves have reached their maximum height or depth, the lines travel away from that point. If the extreme of the curve is allowed to rest on the horizontal guideline, the letter will appear smaller than letters with flat serifs. All letters ending in a point must be drawn with the point a fraction above or below the horizontal guidelines. If the point of a letter is placed directly on the horizontal guidelines, the letter will appear smaller than letters with flat serifs. (Fig. 4).

MS MS

Fig. 4

Rules governing the weight adjustments on single-weight letters are described in detail in the section on Gothic forms. However, the above rules relating to the optical evenness of weight and the placement of curves and points in a line, also apply to the single weight letters.

LETTER PROPORTION

Many treatises on lettering present the relationship of an alphabet to a square, as a device for establishing the relative widths of the letters. Almost invariably, these alphabets are based on the original Roman Capitals and standard lower cases. While this approach may be of minor help to the beginner, I feel that its value is too limited for inclusion here. Many type and lettered forms in use today no longer follow these classic proportions. Flat-sided letters such as News Gothic, Corvinus, Eden, etc. also depart considerably from these basic relative proportions, as do the widely expanded forms.

Lettering is a form of drawing. If one concentrates on holding the *exact* relative proportions by mechanical measurement, with the inevitable overuse of his dividers, the execution of the lettering will be slowed and the caption will lose much of its spontaneous quality.

It's only natural for the beginner to reach out for some method of insuring proper proportions by the use of stated measurements. Some measurements are helpful, of course, but too much reliance upon any system of measurement only serves as a crutch for the beginner and retards the development of his sense of observation. He must learn to *see* and to judge the relative proportion of letters by eye.

An alphabet is largely composed of a set of basic strokes which are joined together, or continued, to produce the shapes of the individual letters. If care is taken to maintain the similarity of these shapes, one has made the major step toward achieving the logical proportions. (Fig. 5).

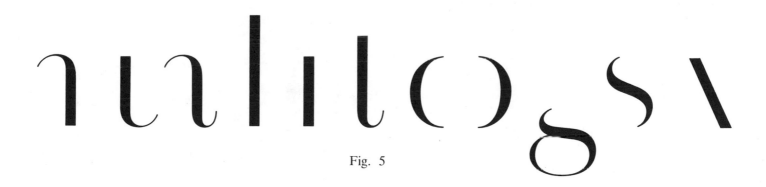

Fig. 5

As a double check, the general relationship of the enclosed or admitted white spaces within the letters must be considered. The actual areas of white space in each letter can't be the same, because of the varying shapes, but any major discrepancy can be detected if the caption is examined for visually obvious holes in the line.

Letters formed by the joining of identical or similar strokes are naturally, identical in width. (Fig. 6). The white spaces in the letters having vertical sides should relate optically to the white spaces within letters which have curved sides.

Fig. 6

b c d e p q

h n u a

This can be accomplished by keeping the enclosed white spaces, in letters which contain curved strokes, a fraction wider at their widest point than the white space allowed between vertical strokes. This is necessary because the white spaces within curved strokes always reduce in width as the curves complete their arc.

Before measuring a letter to establish the width of other letters of the same width, one should study the letter carefully to make sure that it is drawn in a logical proportion. Otherwise all letters in this group will be wrongly proportioned.

The ability to draw letters in their true relative proportion will develop as one learns to observe the correctness of the basic strokes, the relationship of the white spaces, and the rightness of each letter in the area that it occupies.

10

RULES FOR SPACING

It is every bit as important to space letters properly, as it is to draw individual letters correctly. If you letter a line of beautifully drawn characters and space them poorly, you have a line that is far less effective than a caption of mediocre draftsmanship which has been well spaced. Easy readability is the goal, and it can be reached only by drawing letters optically even in weight and properly placed in the line.

With experience, the ability to space letters and words can be developed to the point where measurements with dividers are rarely needed. Spacing is governed by the amount of white space or "air" that is admitted between letters. The varying shapes of the individual letters and the white space admitted into letters, calls for adjustments in the distance allowed between any combinations of these forms.

In time, one should be able to judge these adjustments by eye. The following rules are offered to the beginner, not as a crutch, but as a starting point in his lettering practice.

When the caption has been tentatively sketched in to the given width, examine it carefully for any obvious holes in the spacing. If nothing drastic shows, then the distance between letters that have vertical stems establishes a measurement for spacing. When the average space between these letters has been established, set your dividers to this measurement and use it for the following combinations. Make all these measurements at half the height of the letters.

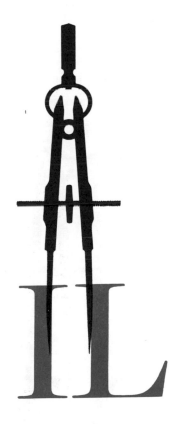 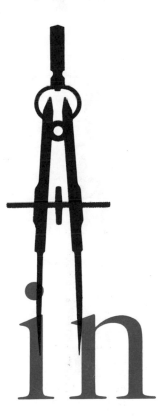

1 Vertical to Vertical

These strokes are the widest apart on your line. Letters with hairline sides must be placed a fraction closer together than the established measurement, as a minor adjustment.

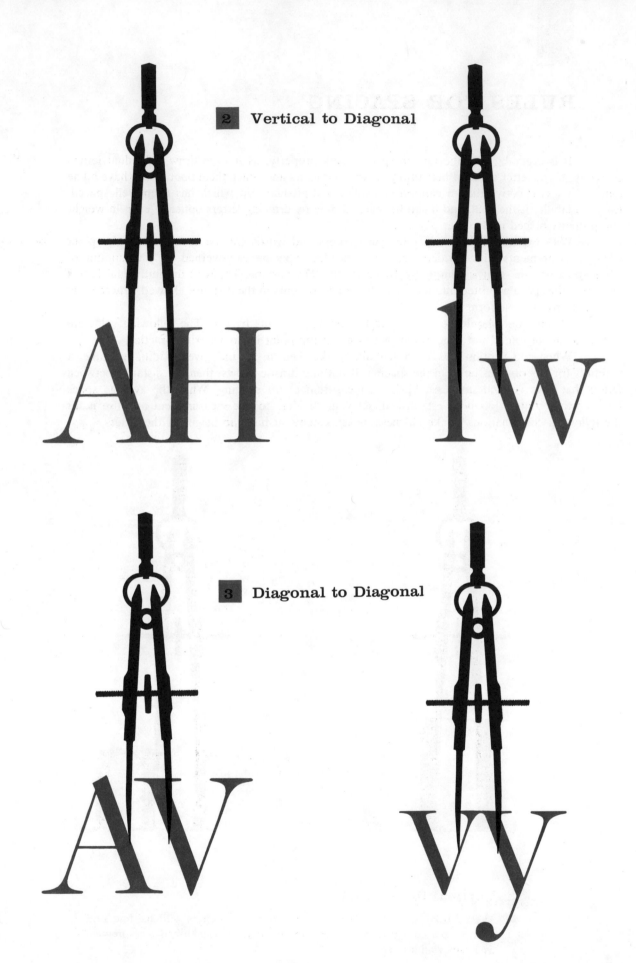

2 Vertical to Diagonal

3 Diagonal to Diagonal

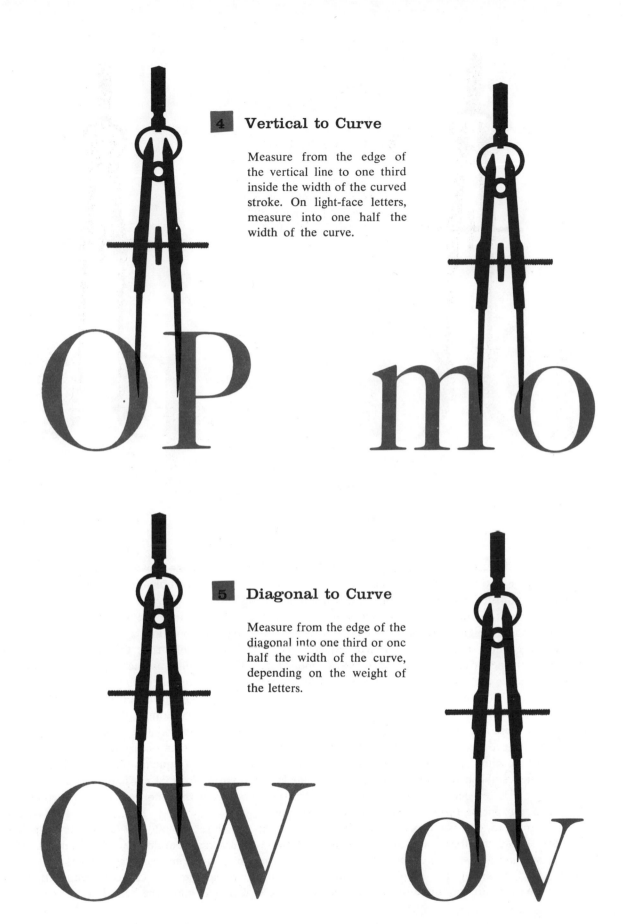

4 Vertical to Curve

Measure from the edge of the vertical line to one third inside the width of the curved stroke. On light-face letters, measure into one half the width of the curve.

5 Diagonal to Curve

Measure from the edge of the diagonal into one third or one half the width of the curve, depending on the weight of the letters.

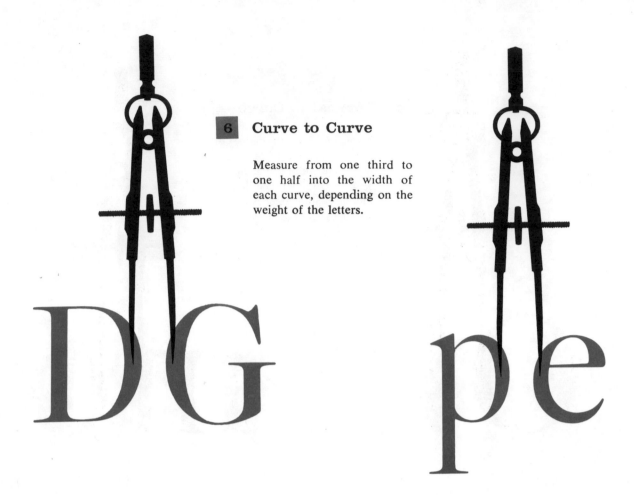

6 Curve to Curve

Measure from one third to one half into the width of each curve, depending on the weight of the letters.

These measurements will be helpful to the beginner, but he must always remember that the eye is the actual judge of correct spacing. There are many combinations of letters that can not be adjusted properly by following a rigid measuring system.

At all times, the admitted white space between letters must be considered as an area that should be enlarged or reduced to correct the spacing. Combinations of letters which admit a lot of white space call for *optical* adjustments. It will help if one tries to visualize the white spaces in negative form or as a mass of tone. (Fig. 7). Combinations such as those shown on these pages are typical of letters which must be spaced with considered judgment.

With the exception of letter-spaced lines—lines in which the characters are spaced widely apart—some mis-spacings are inevitable in the average caption. If the lettering artist allowed these mis-spacings to establish the general spacing of his line, almost all captions would be letter-spaced. Letters with horizontal serifs may be joined together occasionally to reduce the admitted white space, but if this device becomes necessary too frequently in a line, it indicates that the established spacing or proportion of the letters is wrong for that particular caption.

A few letters may be narrowed a fraction more than their normal, relative proportion to ease a spacing problem. These are the lower case r and the capital E, F, L, and T. It is best to use moderation when narrowing these letters. At no time should the letters be crippled, nor should the narrowing appear obvious. If these letters reappear in the same caption, with no spacing adjustment called for, they should be drawn in their normal proportions.

As mentioned above, some mis-spacings are unavoidable. One can only reduce them as best he can, and continue on with the noble feeling that he has made the best of a bad situation.

es Don't crowd the letters this closely.
It's just as bad as no spacing adjustment at all.

rs Placed this tightly, these letters might
bleed together if printed on news stock.
It's an unpleasant eye-catcher
even if this doesn't happen.

Try to visualize the white spaces in negative form or as a mass of tone.

Fig. 7

If the spacing problems are giving you a battle, it's a good idea
to walk away from the job and let it "cool" a bit. (Unless you're
a professional doing a rush job and the art director keeps phoning
to ask, "How much longer?"). In any event, stand back and study
the caption objectively. Forget that the standard rules of spacing
have been observed and try to decide what spacing adjustments
are necessary to make the caption look right to *you*. You're the
judge of spacing, not your dividers.

es

ca es ES Here are pairings of letters that each admit a lot of white space. They can be brought fairly close together when necessary but don't crowd them. There must be a reasonable allowance of white space between the closest strokes of the letters.

ca

ES

rv Here, the kern of the r can be drawn closer to its stem. The outer serif on the weighted diagonal of the v is shortened so that it can be moved in tighter. After that, we're licked.

LA This combination is a lettering man's nightmare. The best we can do to adjust the spacing is never enough. The crossbar of the L may be shortened and the outer serif of the A joined to it in a tight line. Despite this, the LA combination will always be a disrupting factor in a normally spaced line.

CA This is another tough one . . . the C, admitting a mass of white space, followed by the diagonal hairline of the A. Any change of proportion would be too obvious, so the only adjustment we can make is to shorten the outer serif of the hairline and allow it to almost touch the bottom serif on the C. Even if it bleeds shut when reproduced, no great damage will be done to the line.

vy This is a nasty combination . . . two diagonals travelling away from each other! The serifs may be joined closely together and that's all we can do.

LT The crossbar of the L has been tucked under the crossbar of the T. This usually takes care of the spacing problem, but don't interlock them too much.

HOW TO DO IT

Captions lettered for reproduction are generally made larger than reproduction size. It's easier for the lettering artist to draw larger characters and, too, the photoengraver's camera is always kind in cleaning up any raggedness of line when the letters are reduced in size.

Unless the art director has specified a working drawing size, it's up to the lettering artist to decide the size he prefers to letter the caption. Generally, one half larger than reproduction size is workable for the average caption, though some lettering men prefer to work twice size. There are occasions when the reproduction size is so small that the caption must be blown up to three times the size or more.

I have found that any blowup larger than twice size makes it difficult to judge how the general tone of the caption will appear when reduced, and how well the hairlines will hold. It's often better to buckle down with a finer pen and do the letters within a more practical scale-up.

When the layout is given to the lettering artist for finished work, the indication of the caption may range from a rough scrawl, to a meticulous rendering. Many art directors are able letterers, and can give the lettering man a definite idea of what he wants. However, there are instances when any art director, under pressure of time, will make a rough indication and give verbal instructions as to the style and weight he has in mind.

In many large advertising agencies, the lettering on a presentation layout is done comprehensively by a lettering man in the agency's art department and then is given to a lettering specialist for finished work after the client has okayed the layout.

Many agencies send their rough layouts to art studios for comprehensive rendering by the various specialists. In smaller agencies, the art director is often required to render the complete comprehensive layout. It is in this latter group that we most often find varying degrees of indication.

When the finished lettering is to be done by the man who has done the comprehensive lettering on the layout, his problem is considerably eased. If the rendering of the caption has been okayed without radical changes, the most direct step is to get a photostat of the caption blown up to working size and then trace the first tissue from it. This can also be done when the art director or an assistant has lettered a well-indicated caption.

In the case of a roughly scrawled caption, it is advisable to place a tissue over the layout and pencil in the lettering more concisely. This will help the lettering man to judge the relationship of the caption, in its size and weight, to the other elements of the layout. This tissue may then be photostated to a larger size, with the assurance that it will hold its proper place in the advertisement.

Some lettering men prefer to eliminate the cost of photostats by using a reflecting camera or camera lucida for enlarging the caption. This method is sound, if care is taken to avoid distortion.

Here, the lettering indicated in pencil on the layout was photostated up to working drawing size and used for the original trace-off which established the proportion and weight of the finished caption.

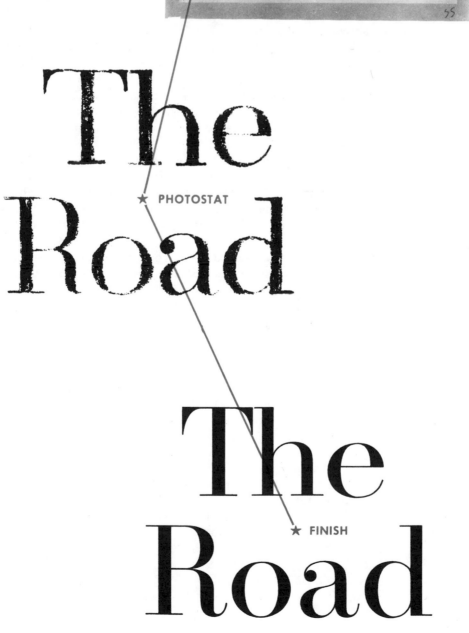

★ PHOTOSTAT

★ FINISH

PREPARATION OF THE TRACING TISSUE

Laying out a commercial caption poses the problem of fitting a given number of characters into lines of specified height and width. First, an experimental "run-through" should be made in fairly rough form to establish the workability of the caption within the specified area. As a rule, the caption can be made to conform to the art director's specifications without radical changes in size, weight, and proportion. However, there are occasions when problems arise that call for compromises with the original layout. It is always advisable, from the standpoint of good business relations, to talk to the art director and explain why these adjustments should be made, and get his opinion on the changes.

I believe that the beginner, who intends to specialize in lettering, should be trained to work to exacting specifications from the start. It is not enough to be able to draw individual letters well. The letters must form a complete caption which fits into its proper place in the entire layout.

At the end of the following chapters dealing with individual alphabets, actual examples of art directors' caption indications are presented, employing the letter style which has been analyzed in that chapter. Some of these examples are carefully pinned down, while others are roughly indicated, typical of the varying degrees of caption indications that the lettering artist is expected to put into finished form. These pages can be used for practice by the beginner. As mentioned in the preceding section, finished lettering is usually made larger than reproduction size. These indications represent "blowups", and the general weight of the letters and the established area must be maintained.

It must be remembered that the art director does not have the time to indicate a caption that presents accurate spacing and standard weight of the letters. It is up to the lettering man to make the spacing adjustments and decide on the average weight required.

The first step is to tape tracing tissue over the rough indication and draw horizontal guidelines, using a T-square, to establish the size of the body of the letters and the height and depth of the ascending and descending strokes.

The first run-through may be made by building up the letters with a soft pencil, B or 2B (Fig. 8) or can be stroked in with a flat sketching pencil. (Fig. 9). However, once the approximate width of the line has been reached, the letters should be built up on subsequent tissue tracings.

First trial run-through

Fig. 8

First trial run-through

Fig. 9

The individual letters need not be drawn too carefully on the first trial run-through. The main object of this tissue is to establish general proportion, the average weight of the letters, and approximate spacing. It would be a waste of time to make a careful drawing of each individual character at this stage, as many adjustments may be necessary on the following trace-offs. The letters should be drawn in a dark tone so that mistakes can be more easily detected. A piece of bond paper, kept under the working hand, will prevent smudging.

If the first lay-in fails to reach a reasonable closeness to the given width, it must be run through again in the same rough form before it can be useful as an underlay for the more carefully rendered second tissue. If the caption is too wide, study the width of the individual characters to decide if they are too expanded. Examine the white spaces between the letters to see if they have been spaced too far apart. Consider the amount of space allowed between the words In a normally spaced line the words need be no further apart than the width of one of the average characters. If the line falls short of the given width, the letters may have been drawn too condensed or too closely spaced.

When the approximate width of line has been reached, the tissue should also be examined upside down and from the reverse side. In these positions, the letters merely form abstract shapes which makes it easier to spot errors in spacing and the general proportion of the letters.

These necessary corrections having been noted, the tissue should be retaped square to the drawing board. A new tissue should be taped over it and the horizontal guide lines retraced. *Although the trial tissue is no longer over the art director's rough, his indication should be kept in view for checking against the developing tissues.*

If one has trouble in drawing the letters on the true vertical (I'm one of the astigmatized group) it will help to draw a set of vertical lines about a half inch apart on each tissue, using the T-square and triangle. A vertical line may be drawn through the center of the balanced curved forms to help in keeping them vertical and symmetrical. If the caption contains italic letters or formal script, a set of guidelines should be drawn on the required diagonal.   (Fig. 10).

Fig. 10

The second run-through must be more carefully executed. The pencil point should be kept sharp in order to produce more concisely drawn letters. Experience will prove that it is faster and more practical to build up the letters freehand. Using the T-square and triangle for preliminary tissues is a painfully slow process and a definite handicap to the development of a spontaneously drawn line.

I strongly recommend that the letters be built up to their weight rather than drawn in outline. It is far more difficult to judge the weight and proportion of an outlined letter. One side of a rigid form should be drawn and then built out to the desired weight. The outer line of the curved forms should be drawn first and filled in to the inside of the stroke. (Fig. 11).

Fig. 11

The experienced lettering man usually reaches his tracing tissue on the second run-through. Beginners may need to retrace the caption several times. Each succeeding tissue should be used as an underlay from which the properly drawn letters are retraced and the necessary corrections in drawing and spacing made. When an adjustment in spacing is necessary, the top tissue should be lifted and moved into the correct position.

The final tissue must be examined with great care before tracing it down. The letter proportions must be checked by analyzing the drawing of the basic strokes and by the amount of white space in and around the letters. If one tries to visualize the enclosed or admitted white spaces as white shapes on a black field, he will be helped in this examination. (Fig. 12).

One should make sure that he has the job licked on the final tissue. After all, it's much easier to erase pencil than ink.

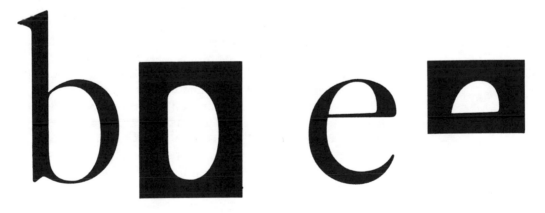

Fig. 12

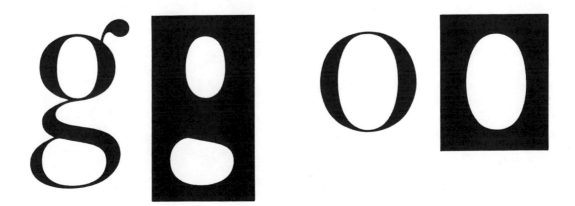

23

TRACING DOWN

When the final tissue has been completed, the reverse side should be blacked with a pencil of medium consistency (preferably a 2H or 3H) and the graphite rubbed smooth with a small piece of tissue or cotton. It is best to avoid the use of a soft pencil for blacking the tissue when the lettering is to be traced onto white paper. When a trace-down is too dark it becomes difficult to see your ink line clearly. A sharp gray line is much easier to follow with the pen. Some lettering artists prefer to rub powdered color or colored chalks on the back of the tissue. The use of color is especially helpful when the lettering is traced on a dark color background. The colors should be applied with cotton and rubbed down hard. All surplus should be brushed away thoroughly to insure a light, crisp line.

The tissue should be taped to the drawing paper at the top only so that it may be lifted while one is tracing to check the accuracy and crispness of the trace-down. A hard, sharp-pointed pencil (6H to 9H) should be used for tracing. The pencil should be sharpened frequently during this process.

After the drawing paper has been thumbtacked square to the drawing board, the horizontal guidelines should be traced first. Be sure to trace the lines that control the height of the capital letters and ascenders, and the depth of the descenders.

There are bound to be occasions when spacing adjustments are still necessary on the final tissue. Rather than redoing a well executed tissue to correct these discrepancies, it's more logical to shift the tissue while tracing. This can be done safely by raising the tissue and drawing horizontal lines on each side of the drawing paper, below the traced guidelines and free of the blacking on the back of the tissue. A short, vertical line is then drawn on one or both of these lines, to show the amount of the corrective opening or closure between letters. When these lines are traced onto the tissue they will serve as a registry for all the necessary shifts. (Fig. 13). Great care must be taken to replace the tissue exactly on the horizontal lines before retaping it to the drawing paper. It's pretty sad to discover that you've traced several characters above or below the guidelines because of a careless replacement of the tissue.

Research Reveals

New Orange

Healthy Discovery

Fig. 13

The first step in the actual trace-down is the tracing of all the rigid horizontal and vertical strokes of the letters. One method of insuring equal width of the vertical stems is to set a pair of small fixed dividers to the average width of the stems and employ them in tracing through. One point of the dividers should be placed lightly against the triangle and the dividers drawn upward, leaning them away from you to avoid cutting through the tissue. (Fig. 14). However, if the dividers are too springy to hold a fixed width under light pressure, their use can be harmful rather than helpful. It will then be safer to trace the verticals through with a pencil, still using the T-square and triangle.

When all the horizontal and vertical lines have been traced through, the paper should be freed from the board. It is easier to trace the curves freehand when the paper can be turned.

Don't hurry your tracing. After spending a lot of time in completing the tissue, it's an awful waste to throw that time away by making a careless trace-down. Keep lifting the tissue to see if the tracing is coming through clearly. (Fig. 15). If any pencil corrections on the drawing paper appear necessary after the tracing is completed, draw them in lightly. Any pressure of the pencil will make an indentation into the paper and make neat inking more difficult. In time one should learn to make these minor corrections with the pen, rather than doing any penciling on the drawing paper.

Fig. 1

Fig. 14

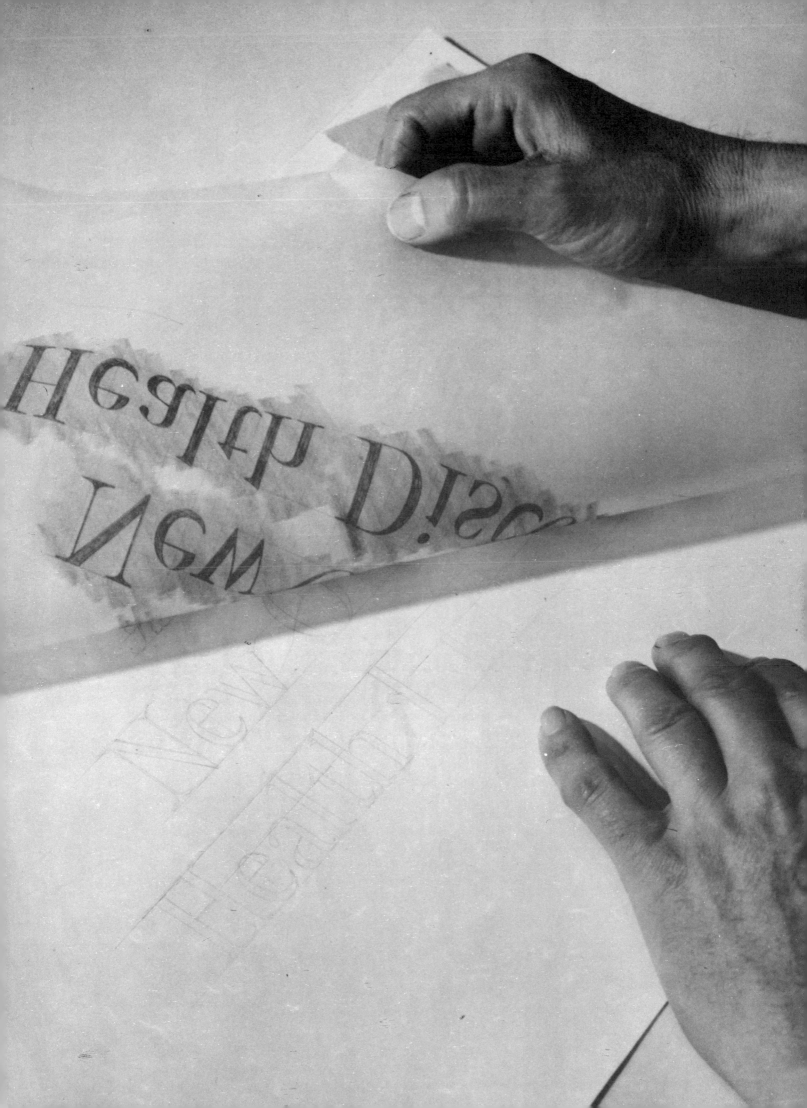

INKING AND WHITING

It is advisable to keep a paper underlay under your hand while inking. Any smudging of the trace down or soiling of the paper surface by moisture or graphite on the hand can be a handicap.

As in penciling, the letters should not be outlined with the pen, but built up to the desired weight—it is just as difficult to gauge the weight of a letter outlined in ink, as it is in pencil. (Fig. 16).

I feel strongly that a beginner should not use a ruling pen and straightedge for the rigid lines until he has developed control of the drawing pen. Until one can draw a reasonably sharp ink line around a curve, it is best to draw all the letters freehand. Otherwise, the caption will be composed of a disturbing combination of sharp, rigid lines and ragged curves. A consistent texture of the edges of all the letters must be maintained on any one caption. For this reason, the Caslon forms are suggested in this book for the initial study. The appearance of these letters is not harmed by an uneven edge, whereas that of crisp letters, such as Bodoni or Gothics, would be.

The pen should be held with a light pressure. "Choking" the penholder will restrict the easy motion of one's hand and can become painful, too, if continued for any length of time.

The pen point must touch the paper lightly, because any amount of pressure will spread the point and scratch the paper surface. When this happens, the pen point will pick up paper fragments, which must be carefully cleaned out before continuing with the lettering. The pen point should be dipped into water often and wiped gently with a soft rag during the entire inking process, to prevent the ink from caking on it. Only a clean pen will draw a clean line.

Inking with fairly short strokes will make for better control. The length of the inking stroke becomes a purely personal technique, often depending on how you feel at the moment. There are days when one may feel especially competent and courageous and can direct the pen with masterful control, and others on which physical causes, or an attack of an inferiority complex—which can beset us all at times—will reduce the length of the strokes to a mere stipple. Experience and results will establish what length of stroke is best for you.

Fig. 16

To avoid flooding, the surplus ink must always be shaken from the pen point after dipping it into the bottle. If the ink does flood in the letter, the corner of a blotter should be dipped into the puddle to drain it off before completing the letter.

Some lettering artists prefer to work toward an edge at all times, first drawing one side of the letter and then reversing the paper to fill in toward the other edge. While I do not disparage this method, and often use it when the paper surface is fighting the pen, I believe that the ability to back up to an edge with the pen will speed up the execution, and should be practiced diligently.

Drawing the curved strokes is made easier by turning the paper as one rounds the curve, but the amount of turning can be reduced with practice, too.

For the inking of flat serifs, it is best to turn the caption sideways and draw the line downward. (Fig. 17).

Mistakes should be ignored until the entire caption has been inked. (This statement brings to mind a friend of mine who jokingly claimed that when his pen slips on the first letter, that establishes the weight of his line!). While the temptation to clean up slips of the pen as they are made is natural for the beginner, it is hardly the professional attitude. The execution of the line will be slowed and the white paint used to correct the error is likely to get dirty before the caption is completed.

When the line has been inked in and thoroughly dry, the pencil lines should be erased with art gum. It should then be checked carefully to see if any cleaning up can be done with ink. One should try to make as many corrections as he can with ink and not rely too much on white paint. The caption should be turned upside down for study of the curved lines and the general color of the line. It's often helpful to use a pen with a finer point for the corrections with ink.

The white paint should be mixed to a creamy consistency in a porcelain palette. After the brush is dipped into the paint, it should be twirled on the underlay paper to bring it to a fine point.

The white paint should cover the ink without much overpainting. Trial and experience will help to decide the right consistency. The brush must be washed out regularly while working to prevent the paint from caking at the ferrule. The whiting strokes should be kept as narrow as possible, which can be accomplished by working with the point of the brush only and with no dragging of the brush along the letters. A wide whiting stroke does not necessarily damage the reproduction of a caption, but it does detract from its general appearance when it is presented to the art buyer.

Naturally, some mistakes might be made with the white brush, too. These should be corrected with lampblack, rather than ink, which tends to crack off when used over white paint. The lampblack must be kept in a fairly thick consistency to prevent any flooding over the white paint. Many a beginner, before his brush control has developed, may suffer the irritating experience of making errors with his lampblack, which then calls for more white, then lampblack again, etc., a process which can result in an unplanned piece of embossing. However, control of the brush and pen will develop with lots of practice.

Fig. 17

THE CASLON LETTERS

THE CASLON LETTERS

Designed by William Caslon in 1734, these alphabets have survived the critical test of time. Although innumerable alphabets have appeared since the introduction of these forms, the Caslons have held their rightful place among the most widely used type faces for body text.

There have been periods in which the use of Caslons for main captions, in type or hand-lettered form, was neglected, but they have invariably been brought back to favor by discriminating art directors and typographers. They are generally considered to be one of the most readable forms in existence today.

A study of many subsequent type faces will show that Caslon has had a considerable influence upon their design. Once a student has learned to draw Caslon letters, he will find it easier to analyze the construction of contemporary alphabets based on the "Humanistic" forms. I consider Caslon to be the grandfather of many of these alphabets.

The lower-case letters are not easy to draw correctly at the start, but if a student sincerely wants to learn about lettering, he will find that this initial study will be to his advantage.

When William Caslon designed his first type faces, he was influenced by the existing types of his day. These faces were developments of the letters which were drawn with the flat pen or quill for the handwritten manuscripts and books preceding the invention of movable type.

The construction of lower-case letters is more easily seen in the light of this relationship to the flat pen renderings. Once this is recognized, the reasons for the off-center distribution of the weights in most of the curves and the subtle shapes of the turns will become more obvious. When the student has learned *why* the letters are so formed, his problem of drawing the letters correctly is simplified.

Originally, all the hand lettering in European manuscripts and books were lettered in capitals based on the Roman Capitals, which were incised in stone over two thousand years ago. These letters are the ancestors of our modern renderings of capital-letter forms.

As the public's interest in books grew, it became necessary to develop more speed in the production of hand-drawn letters. By experimentation, the writers developed the "Uncial" letters, a combination of capital and lower-case forms which could be rendered more quickly because they required less lifting of the pen from the paper. In time, as further experiments were made to reduce the number of strokes on a letter, other changes in letter forms developed. The partial use of capitals was considerably reduced in a resultant style called the "semi-uncials." Eventually, letters called "minuscules," with all the capital forms eliminated, became the accepted style for body text. These minuscules are the ancestors of our lower-case forms.

Examples of the uncials, semi-uncials and minuscules on Plates 1, 2 and 3, show the gradual evolution toward our present forms.

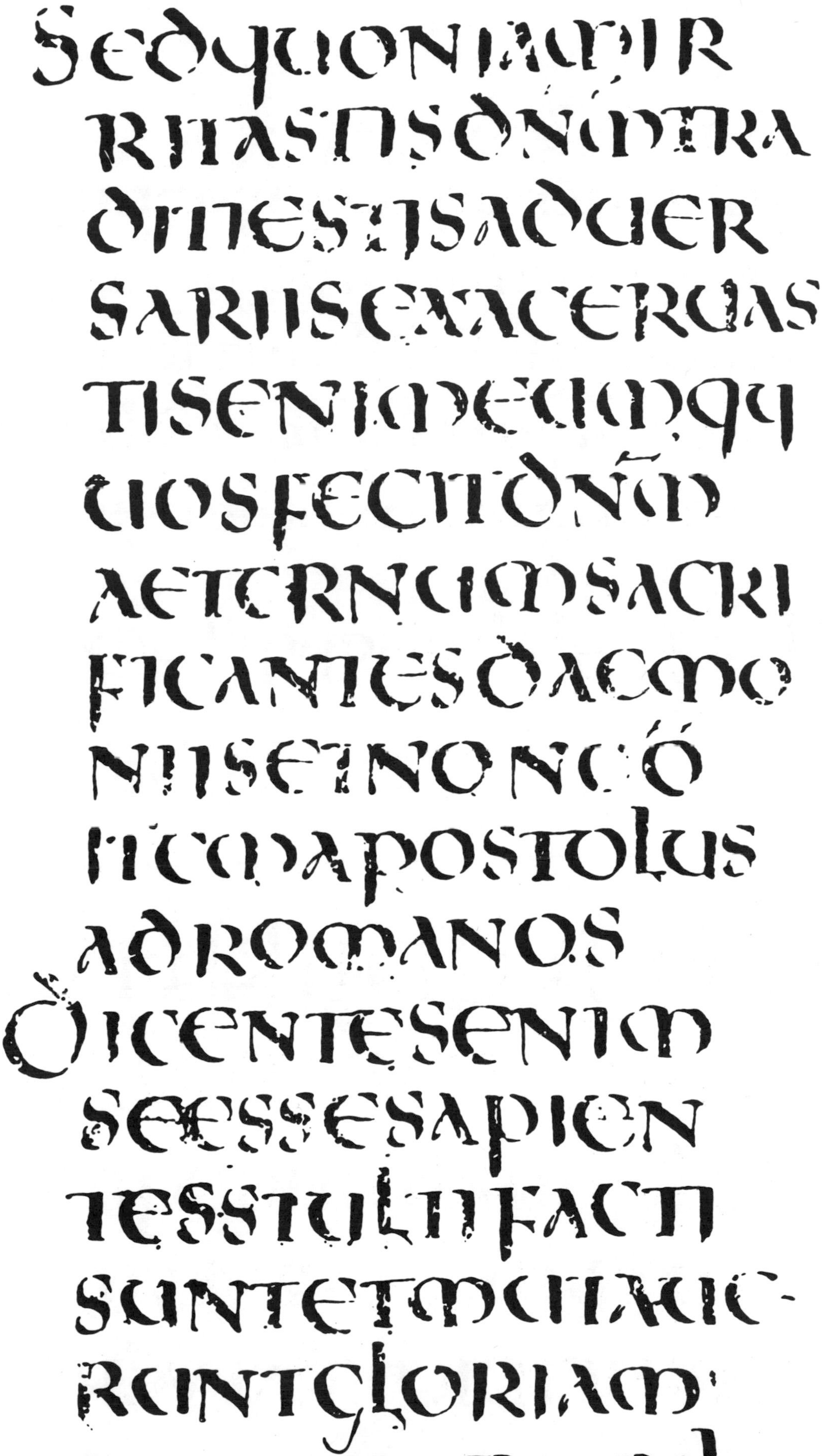

SEDQUONIAMUIR
RITASIISDNICONTRA
OMNESIISADUER
SARIISEXACERUAS
TISENIMEUNQU
UIOSFECITDNM
AETERNUMSACRI
FICANTESDAEMO
NIISETNONDO
IICMAPOSTOLUS
ADROMANOS
DICENTESENIM
SEESSESAPIEN
TESSTULTIFACTI
SUNTETMUTAUE
RUNTGLORIAM
INCORRUPTIBILIS

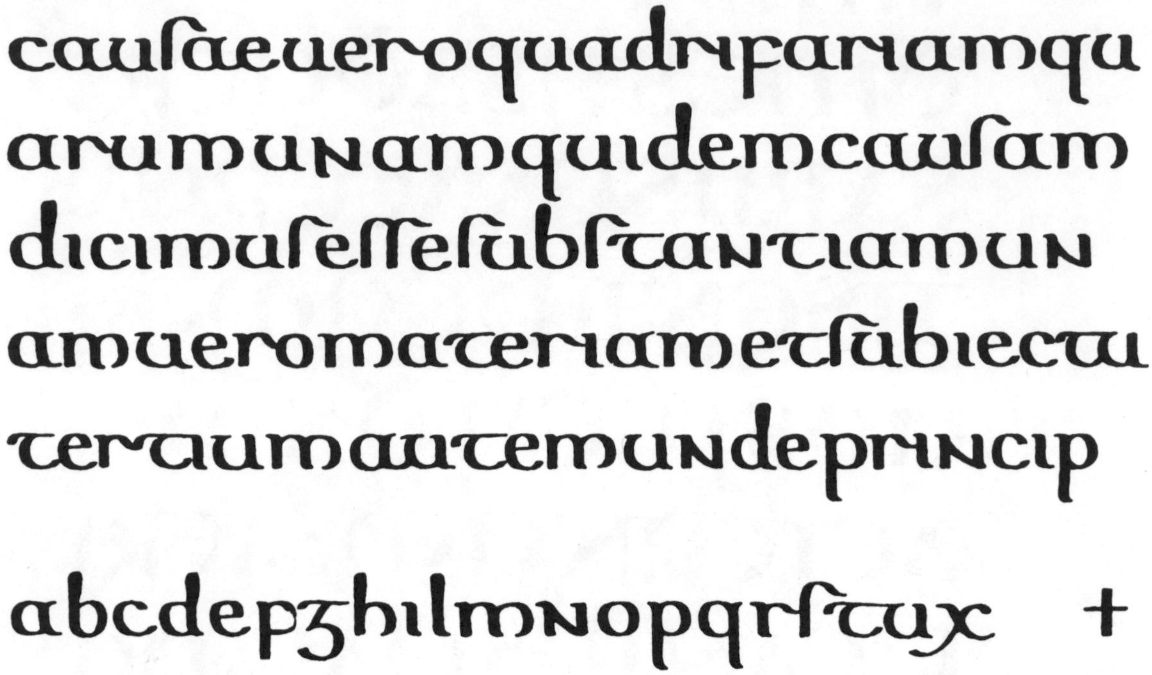

causaeueroquadrifariamqu

arumunamquidemcausam

dicimuseffesubstantiamun

amueromateriametsubiectu

tertiumautemundeprincip

abcdepzhilmnopqrstux   †

Plate 2
Examples of uncial letters

ABCDEFGHIJKLMNOP
QRSTUVWXYZ&
abcdefghijklmnopqrstuvw
xyz&!?:,;, –.123456789
·IN PRINCIPIO ERAT VERBUM·

36

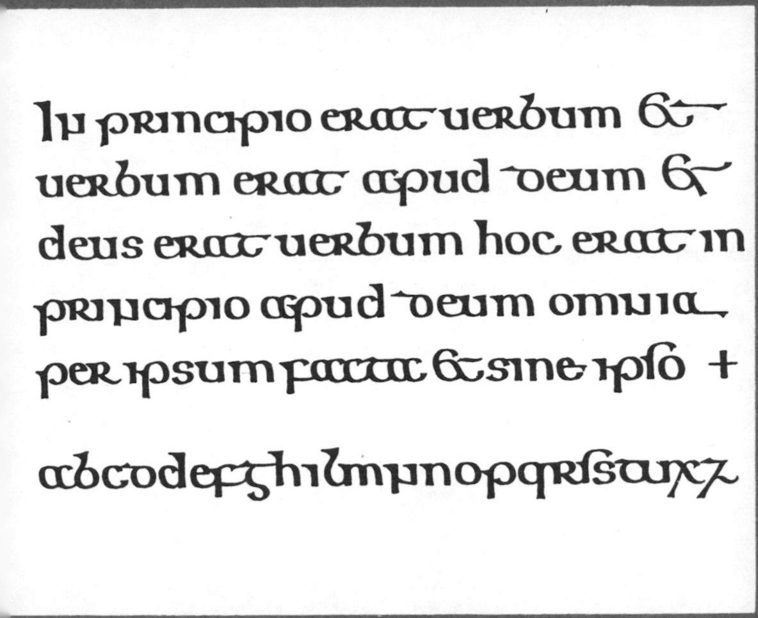

In principio erat uerbum &
uerbum erat apud deum &
deus erat uerbum hoc erat in
principio apud deum omnia
per ipsum facta & sine ipso +

abcdefghilmnopqrstuxz

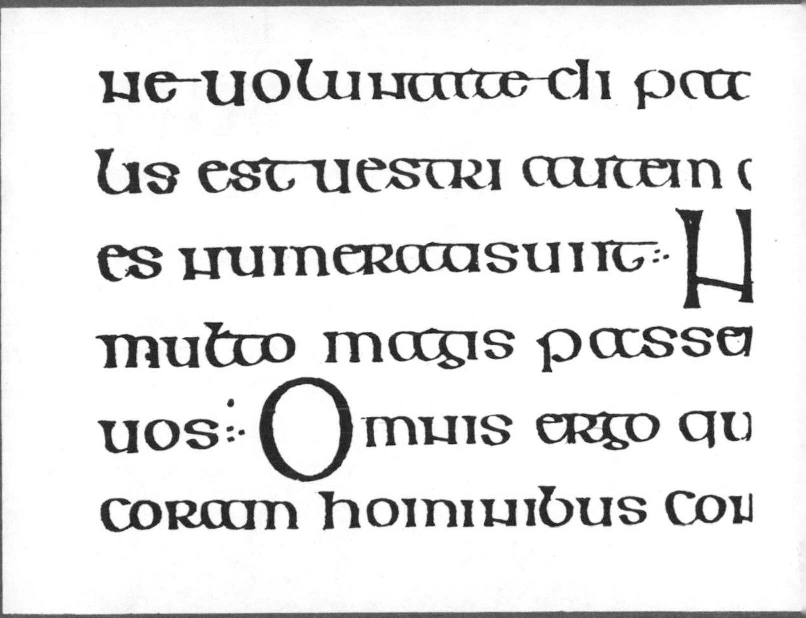

ne uoluntate di pat
lis est uestri cautein (
es humeratasuit: H
multo magis passe
uos: O mnis ergo qu
coram hominibus con

Plate   3

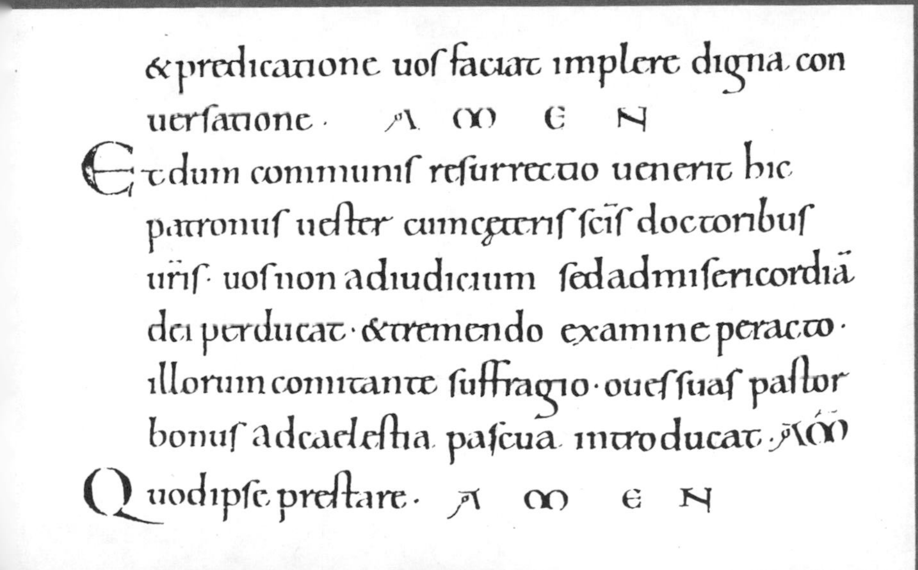

& predicatione uos faciat implere digna con
uersatione .   A   M   E   N
Et dum communis resurrecio uenerit hic
patronus uester cumceteris scis doctoribus
uris· uos non adiudicium sed admisericordia
dei perducat· & tremendo examine peracto·
illorum comitante suffragio· oues suas pastor
bonus ad caelestia· pascua· introducat· AMEN
Quod ipse prestare· A   M   E   N

Minuscule letters

Minuscules similar to
present day calligraphy

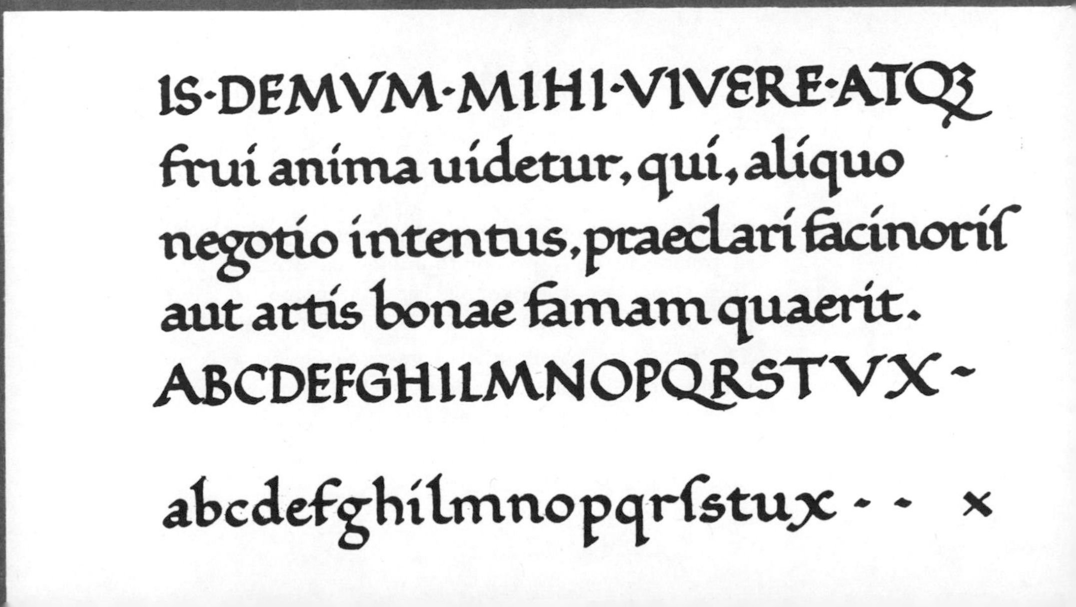

IS·DEMVM·MIHI·VIVERE·ATQ3
frui anima uidetur, qui, aliquo
negotio intentus, praeclari facinoris
aut artis bonae famam quaerit.
ABCDEFGHILMNOPQRSTVX ~

abcdefghilmnopqrstux · · ·   x

FLAT PENCIL RENDERINGS

The best and quickest way to the understanding of Caslon forms is to begin by stroking out the letters with a flat, chiseled pencil. By this method, one is able to see in his *own* letters why the shapes and distribution of weights were followed in the type, and will be able to actually *see* the construction of type and lettered forms.

Fig. 18

The practice should begin with the basic strokes (Fig. 18). It is best to work with just a few sheets of tracing tissue taped or thumbtacked over the board covering, as a firm surface is needed to produce strokes of even tone. Using the complete tissue pad will cause the tissue to buckle under the pressure of the pencil, making it difficult to maintain even pressure.

The basic strokes should be practiced until one is able to draw the straight lines and curved strokes crisply. It will be easier to draw the basic strokes large, at the start.

Fig. 19

A 4B sketching pencil should be used, with the graphite kept at its full width and sharpened to a chisel edge on the sandblock.   (Fig. 19).

The pencil must be held firmly on a slight angle.   (Fig. 20).

FRONT VIEW   **SIDE VIEW**   **FRONT VIEW**

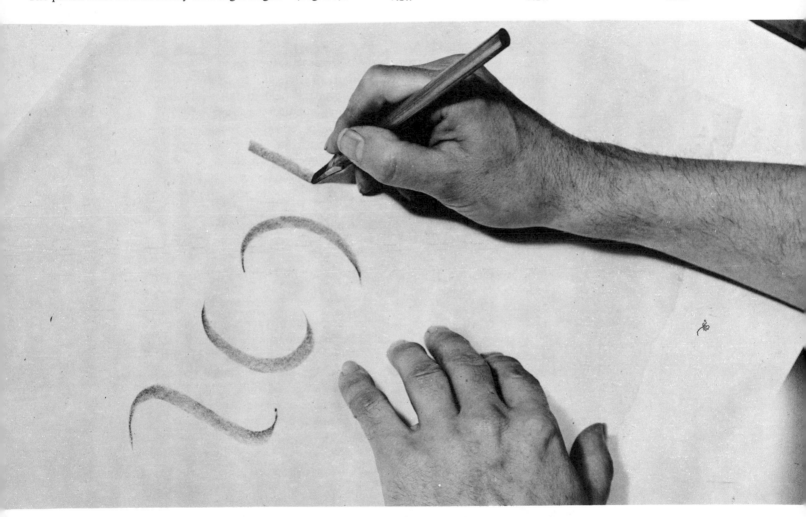

Fig. 20

Flat turns on the curved strokes will be avoided by moving the forearm while drawing these large strokes, rather than using the wrist and fingers only.

Yes, I know that the graphite will break often during this exercise! There are times when I'm sure that the sketching pencil I'm using came from a crate that was thrown from the top of a boxcar during shipment. The annoyance of stopping to sharpen the pencil frequently can be eased by sharpening several pencils before beginning to work.

After considerable practice on the basic strokes, the beginner should be ready to tackle the complete letters. The letters, too, should be drawn large at the start. With the graphite held to full width, a body height of 1½ inches will produce a letter of average weight. Horizontal guidelines should be drawn to control the height, with enough space between these sets of lines to allow for the ascenders and descenders of the letters. The sequence of strokes shown on Plate 4 should be followed. Several complete alphabets should be stroked out in large size, using the thin edge of the pencil for hairlines and serifs.

The letter "O" and the small "o" which comprise part of the g are exceptions to the rule of off-balance weights in Caslon, and are lettered with symmetrically balanced weights. However, for this exercise it is not necessary to draw this symmetry. Use the basic curve strokes and allow the weights to fall as these strokes produce them.

When sufficient practice has begun to produce the large letters in reasonably accurate form and proportion, the height of the letters can be reduced to ¾ inch. A 2B sketching pencil can be used for these smaller letters, with the graphite sanded down evenly on each side to approximately half of its width. (Fig. 19). At this point, one should begin to practice the stroke-out of words, rather than an alphabet sequence, in order to get the "feel" of letter spacing.

a b c d e

f g h i j k

l m n o p

q r s t u v

Plate 4

w x y z

ANALYSIS of letter construction

When several alphabets have been stroked out in both sizes, compare your renderings with the examples shown on Plate 5.

Note that the natural strokings tend to produce flatter curves than on the type forms. (Plate 6). These strokes are indicated by a red line on the letters a, h, m, n, and u. Most lettering artists draw this flatter curve, which adds crispness to the caption.

A red line has been drawn at the widest part of the curves on the letters a, b, c, d, e, p, and q. If your own stroke-outs have been properly executed, following the basic curve strokes, the weights will be similarly distributed. The greatest weights on the curves of the a, c, d, e, and q occur below the mathematical center of the curve, while the reverse strokes have placed the greatest weight of the curve on the b and p above the mathematical center.

Having drawn the off-balance distribution of weights on your own stroke-outs, the placement of these weights should be easily remembered and understood. The proper placement of weights is essential to the drawing of the Caslon lower cases.

By executing the return strokes joining the stem to the curve on the letters b, d, p, and q as noted by red arrows, you have demonstrated why William Caslon placed weights at these points.

Note that the curves of the h, m, n, and u follow the more crisp turn of the curve into the stem at the top of the a, as against the softer turn on the same letters in the type alphabet.

The flat instrument tends to produce a wider, more graceful sweep from the stem of the a, similar to that of the t.

The forward curve from the top of the e descends more abruptly than on the type e.

The center curving stroke on the s, after reaching its full weight, maintains even weight in a gentle downward curve until it diminishes around the right hand curve.

a b c d e

f g h i j k

l m n o p

q r s t u v

Plate 5

w x y z

a b c d e

f g h i j k

l m n o p

q r s t u v

w x y z

Plate 6

Caslon 540 type

44

a b c d e

f g h i j k

l m n o p

q r s t u v

w x y z

Plate 7

Hand-lettered Caslon

After stroking out the larger letters, one should practice drawing them in progressively smaller sizes until he can clearly indicate letters in the sizes which are more often required for advertising captions and sub-captions.

ANALYSIS of finished lower case forms

In my opinion, the lettering student is handicapped by the use of type as his only copy when he begins his study of most Roman forms. Considerable study of the type forms, will, in time, suggest reasonable adjustments in the transition to hand-lettered forms. However, the process can be speeded by a careful comparison of type to hand lettering at the beginning of the study. The original type designs should never be ignored. A student must be thoroughly familiar with them before he can recognize a good hand-lettered interpretation.

In following type faces alone, the beginner's first efforts will inevitably result in a poorly executed copy of the type. Until he develops more control of his pen and brush, he cannot hope to better a type-set caption by using type forms as copy. The aim of lettering artists should always be to add to, or improve upon, type. If we do not, the typographers will catch up with us and we'll be out of business.

With the exception of the New Caslon series and the bold faces, Caslon types are beautifully formed. The lettering artist should use restraint in drawing his own interpretation of the letters. However, some adjustments can be made that will help the general color and spacing of a caption. All type designs are governed by the rigid restrictions imposed by the width of the font, a factor which causes inevitable mis-spacings in all lines that do not allow for letter-spacing. The frequent necessity for close line-spacing has dictated the height of ascenders and depth of descenders. The lettering man is not restricted in this respect. He may use taller ascenders and deeper descenders, when line-spacing allows, and make all necessary adjustments for correct spacing.

Actual practice on the letters should be preceded by a careful comparison of the examples of Caslon 540 type on Plate 6 with the conservatively lettered alphabet on Plate 7.

The numbered arrows on Plate 8 indicate the changes made in the lettered alphabet.

These changes are described in the numbered paragraphs below, including the points of design in the type which should always be held in the lettered forms.

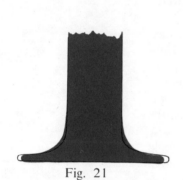

Fig. 21

Photostat blow-up of type serif. Overlay shows sharper curve into serifs on hand lettering

Fig. 22

1 All ascenders and descenders have been lengthened. Their length is elastic in the hand-lettered forms and is governed only by logical proportion and line spacing.

2 The flatter curve, as produced by the flat pencil renderings, has been employed on the h, m, n, and u. These curves are the same as the curve on the top of the a.

3 The horizontal serifs turn more crisply into the stems as compared to the softer sweep on the type. (Fig. 21). The triangular serifs are identical to the type, forming an equilateral triangle if completed through the stems. This also applies to the larger triangle on the t. (Fig. 22).

4 The weight of the return stroke joining the lobes to the stems at the bottom of the b and p and at the top of the d and q has been reduced.

5 The sweep from the stem of the a is drawn wider, similar to the t.

6 The shape of the kern of the c is drawn the same as the kern of the a.

7 The hairline crossbar of the e is dropped lower to produce a better balance of white space. The forward curve on the top arcs downward more abruptly than the extended curve of the type e.

8 A wider curve has been drawn at the top of the f. This change is optional as the design of the type f works well in hand-lettering. The crossbar has been thinned slightly, though it is still thicker than the weight of the hairlines and serifs.

9 The small "o" on the g has been drawn in a taller oval shape. The descending sweep is sent deeper to allow for a more graceful curve. The ear on the small "o" may be placed higher on the oval.

10 The dots on the i and j are placed closer to the letters. The wider curve on the bottom of the j is optional.

a b c d e f g

h i j k l m n

o p q r s t u

v w x y z

Plate 8

49

11 The hairline diagonal on the k meets the stem at a lower point for a more balanced distribution of white space. As on the type, the tail of the k extends further forward than the hairline diagonal.

12 The m and w should be drawn narrower than the type forms to hold more even color on a line by reducing the admitted white space.

13 The "O" and the small "o" on the g have symmetrically balanced weights.

14 The center sweep of the s has been lowered for a more balanced distribution of white space. However, more white space is still allowed below the center sweep for optical balance. As on the type, the curve on the belly of the s extends a fraction beyond the top serif.

15 The weight of the crossbar of the t may be narrowed, but is still drawn thicker than the weight of the hairlines and serifs.

16 The bottom crossbar of the z has been shortened to an optical balance with the top right-hand point.

17 The diagonals on the x cross at a point above the mathematical center of its height, making it wider at the base and allowing more white space below the crossing.

The letters without numbered arrows are drawn the same as the type with the exception of the minor changes on the serifs.

Until the beginner has developed his skill in pen handling, all the Caslon forms should be inked in freehand, using the methods shown in the "How To Do It" section. At this stage, it is best to letter a caption in which the letter edges are similar in technique. Most lettering specialists agree that the use of a ruling pen, at any time, detracts from the beauty of the Caslon forms. However, we have to face the fact that rush jobs occur often in the advertising business and that the ruling pen does speed the inking process. A compromise can be made by using a regular drawing pen, held against a straightedge. The drawing pen will produce an edge with a minute texture, rather than the hard line made with a ruling pen.

Caslon lower cases do not lend themselves to expansion, but may be drawn in moderately condensed form without too great a loss of the characteristics and grace of the letters.

Air power is peace power

Tremendously important

He'll love you *both-if*

Westinghouse

CAPITALS

As mentioned earlier, the Roman capitals originally incised in stone, (Fig. 24) formed the basis for our modern capitals. Their general design and proportion has been. followed in numerous alphabets.

When the early manuscript writers drew these letters on paper, using flat pens, the alphabet became known as Square Capitals (Fig. 23). A comparison of these letters to the Caslon type alphabet on Plate 9 will show the influence they exerted on William Caslon's designs. However, he obviously added his own artistry to his interpretation of the written forms.

In the hand lettering of Caslon capitals, the type characteristics are generally held. The major adjustments are made to achieve a more even color in the line than can be accomplished with type. These adjustments are made by narrowing the widest letters of the alphabet which enclose or admit the most white space.

Fig. 23

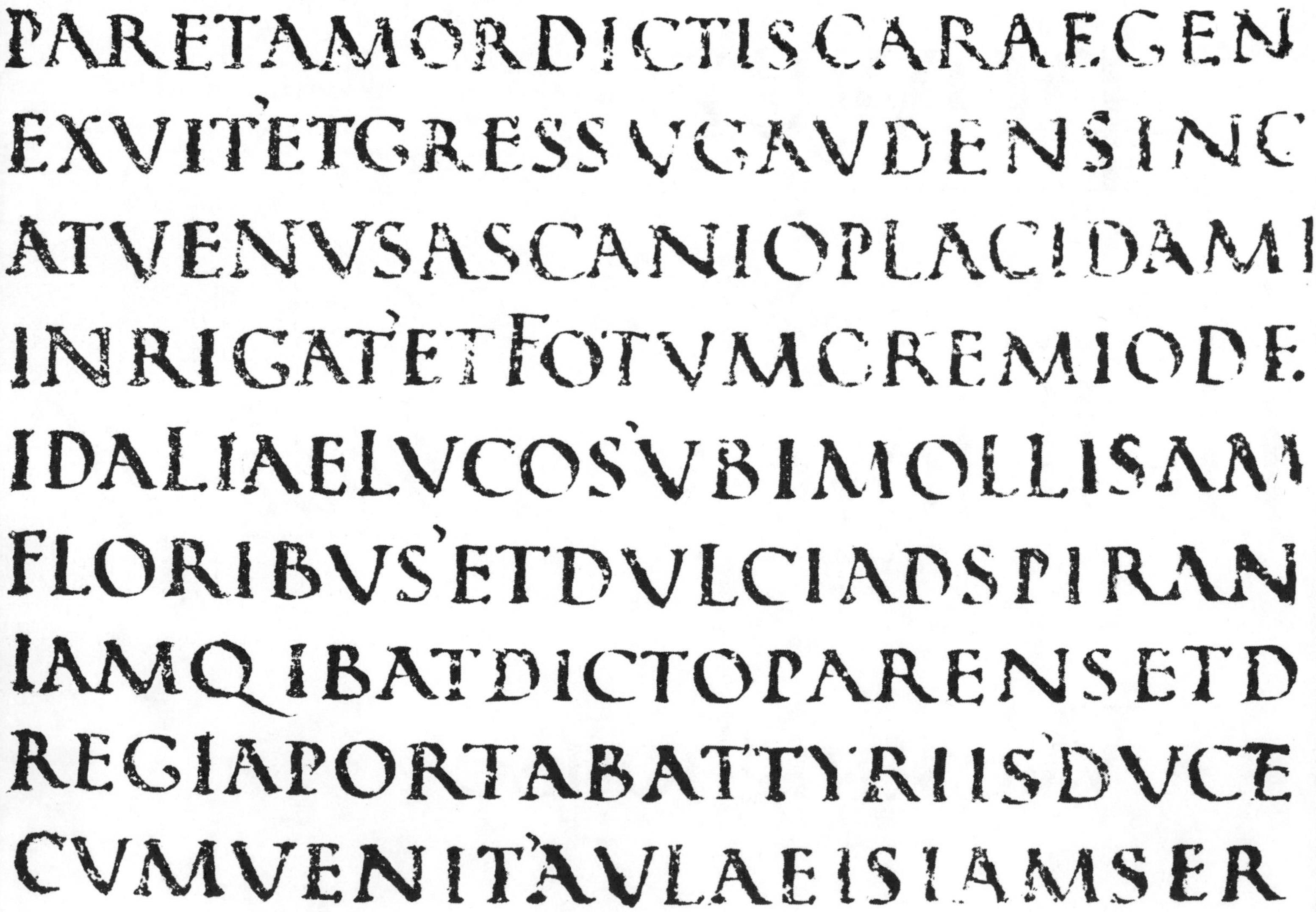

PARETAMORDICTISCARAEGEN
EXVITETGRESSVGAVDENSINC
ATVENVSASCANIOPLACIDAMI
INRIGATETFOTVMCREMIODE.
IDALIAELVCOSVBIMOLLISAM
FLORIBVSETDVLCIADSPIRAN
IAMQIBATDICTOPARENSETD
REGIAPORTABATTYRIISDVCE
CVMVENITAVLAEISIAMSER

ABCDE
FGHIK
LMNO
PQRST
UVW
XYZ.J

Fig. 24

The numbered arrows on Plate 9 indicate the changes made in the lettered alphabet. To avoid the confusion of too many arrows, in cases where the changes apply to a considerable number of letters, the arrow points to one letter on which the change occurs. The numbered paragraphs below, list all the letters on which the same changes have been made. They also include specific points of design in the type, which should always be held in the lettered forms.

1 The serifs turn more crisply into the weighted stems than the softer curve on the type. However, the serifs which complete the hairline strokes, carry a heavier weight similar to the type serif.

2 The lower lobe of the B has been narrowed, but still extends further than the top lobe. Likewise, the K is drawn wider at the bottom and the tail of the R extends beyond its lobe. Note that the tail of the R is not rigid, but curves gently toward its serif.

3 The letters drawn narrower than the type forms are the C, D, G, H, L, N, O, Q, T, and U. The L is often narrowed more than the other letters when preceding an A. The M rarely calls for narrowing because the inner diagonals break up the admitted white space within the letter.

4 The top crossbar of the F may be drawn a fraction narrower than the top crossbar of the E, so that it can be placed closer to the following letter, thereby reducing the admission of white space below the center crossbar. The bottom crossbars of the E and Z have been shortened for the same reason.

5 The angle of the serifs on the E, F, L, T, and Z are drawn with a less acute angle than the angle of the type serifs, to allow for closer spacing when necessary.

6 Unlike the lower-case letters, the weights of the curves on the capitals are all symmetrically balanced. While it is commendable to try to draw these curves as geometrically correct as possible, it is best to avoid drawing pencil structures to insure their balance. One should be able to hold a reasonably balanced curve by drawing a vertical pencil line through the center of the O and Q and if needed, through other letters containing curves.

7 The curves from the rigid stems into the lobes of the B, D, P, R, and into the crossbars of the E and L have been reduced in weight.

8 The middle crossbars in the B, E, F, H, and R are drawn a fraction above the center of the letters.

9 The change of design on the tail of the Q is optional.

A B C D E F

G H I J K L

M N O P Q R

S T U V W X

Y Z & & ? ?

Plate 9   55

A B C D E F
G H I J K L
M N O P Q R
S T U V W X

Plate 10

Caslon 540 type—capitals

Y Z ? &

A B C D E F

G H I J K L

M N O P Q R

S T U V W X

Plate 11

Hand-lettered Caslon capitals

Y Z & & ? ?

57

Basic strokes of Caslon capitals

Caslon Capitals lose much of their grace when lettered in boldface. When a heavy weight is needed in a caption, it is best to employ other letter forms especially designed for bold display.

Before beginning the build-up of these letters, it is advisable to practice them in stroke-out form as shown on Plate 12. Students who plan to become layout men will especially benefit by a great deal of stroke-out practice.

When stroking out the lobes of the B, P, and R, and the curved strokes of the C, D, G, O, and Q, the flat pencil should be held horizontal to the guidelines, as the weighted curves of the capitals distribute their weight symmetrically. On all other strokes, the pencil should be held on a slight angle as on the lower cases.

Triangular serifs may be two-stroked to produce the general effect of a triangle.

ABCDE
FGHIJK
LMNOP
QRSTU
VWXYZ

Plate 12

"This Mobilgas Special advertisement for General Petroleum Corporation was lettered in its entirety by Mort Leach. Basic design was done by Bill Tara; the agency, Stromberger, LaVene, McKenzie, Los Angeles. The ad gained considerable favorable comment in the trade, but, more important, produced exceptional readership from the public at large. A survey using the standard readership techniques proved that the ad was noted by 60 per cent, seen-associated by 47 per cent, and achieved a read-most figure of 14 per cent. The client and the agency regarded this read-most figure as being remarkably high and felt that it reflected the readers' awareness of the care exercised in the layout and lettering. This ad appeared in 196 daily newspapers in the seven Western states in April, 1954."

T. L. Stromberger

ITALICS—LOWER CASE

Italic type forms, first produced in Italy at the beginning of the 16th century, were developments of the slanted hand-written cursive scripts of that period. (Fig. 25). Their early popularity was due to the fact that they were economical forms to use, as the condensed letters allowed more words to a page.

In present-day advertising, italics are often used to accent a statement. They also serve in adding a change of pace in a caption that might otherwise present a monotonous appearance. Their use also offers a practical solution to the problem of getting a lot of copy into a small area.

When studying the construction of the letters, it must be kept in mind that the Caslon italics, also, are based on the humanistic writings. The basic strokes follow the effects produced by a flat pen.

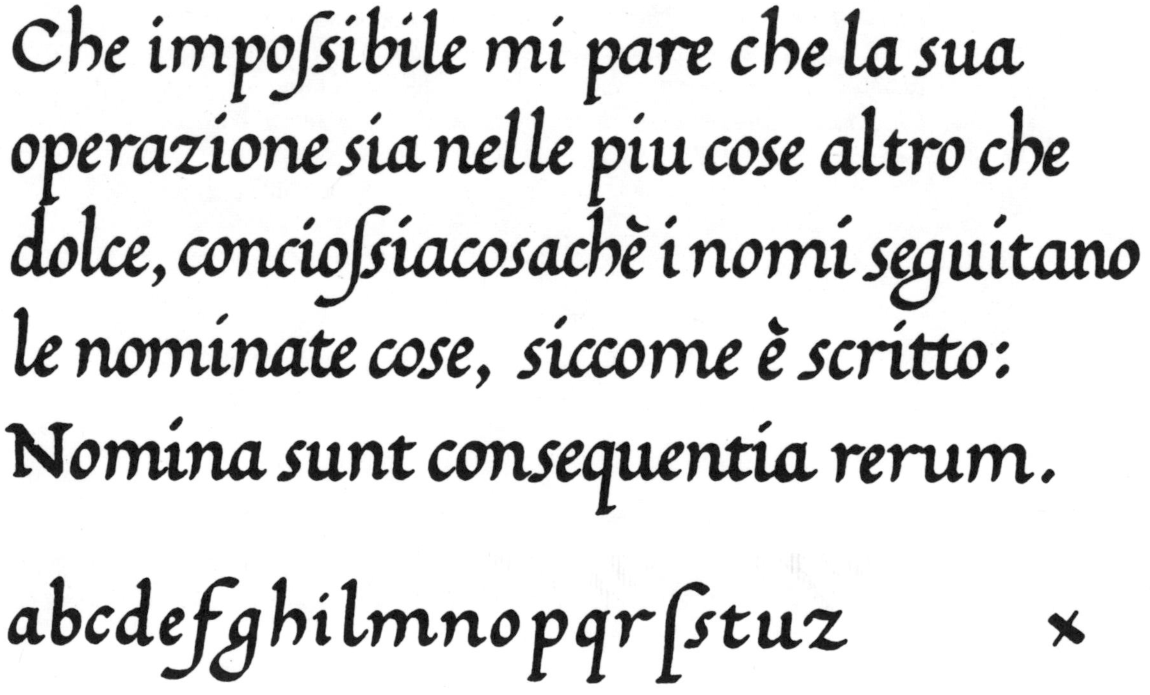

Che impoſsibile mi pare che la sua operazione sia nelle piu cose altro che dolce, concioſsiacosachè i nomi seguitano le nominate cose, siccome è scritto: Nomina sunt consequentia rerum.

abcdefghilmnopqrſstuz ×

Fig. 25

General Motors Dealers

for their determination to deliver the finest service in the automobile industry

Found...in fresh oranges...

different health factor...

As on the preceding alphabets, the red arrows point to the changes made in the lettered forms, Plate 13, compared to the type faces on Plate 14, and to the type construction which must be held on the lettered forms.

1 Both the type and hand-lettered italics distribute the greatest weight on the curves of the a, c, d, e, and q below the center of the stroke. This is accomplished by drawing the inner curve on the same diagonal as the rigid lines, while the outer curve follows a sharper diagonal. (Fig. 26).

2 The greatest weight of the curves of the b and p appears above the center of the stroke.

3 The hairlines on the lobes, with the exception of the p, flow smoothly into the rigid lines to produce the oval shape of the enclosed white space. (Fig. 27). Note that the oval is a narrow shape. By observing the shape and width of the enclosed white space, the frequent tendency to expand these letters will be avoided.

4 The curving hairlines which join the stems at the top of the a, d, and q do not dip deeply into the stems. All other hairlines joining or departing from the stems, sweep more deeply into the stems at the top of the letters and higher into the stems at the bottom. (Fig. 28).

5 The shape of the curve from the stems into the hairlines should be studied carefully. These are not the balanced curves which appear in many other italic forms, but instead, take a sharper turn that produces a somewhat "pointed" arc. (Fig. 26). Some lettering men choose to modify this brisk turn, but the general characteristics of the type design should be held. The hairlines should arc away from the stems, as if they were travelling toward a connection with the adjoining letters, rather than running parallel to the stems.

6 The right hand stems of the h, m, n, and the left hand stems of the u and the simplified y and w are drawn on a slightly sharper diagonal to correct the illusion of their widening at the open end, caused by the turn into the hairline. (Fig. 29). On the type, the stems of these letters are parallel and the illusion of widening at the bottom of the letters is obvious.

7 The length of the descenders and ascenders is elastic, depending only upon their logical relationship to the body of the letters.

8 The hand-lettered x is generally lettered with the oval kerns. This change is optional.

9 The dots on the i and j are drawn closer to the letters.

10 The y in the type forms does not follow the optical slant of the rest of the letters. This has been adjusted in the lettered y.

64

abcdefg

hijklmn

opqrstu

vwxy

Plate 13
Hand-lettered Caslon italics lower case

zzzyvw

65

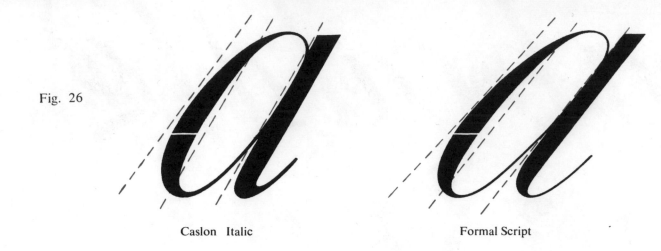

Fig. 26

Caslon Italic   Formal Script

Based on the action of the flexible pen which effected the weight distribution on the earlier script letters, the weights on the Caslon Italic curves are placed below the mathematical center of the height of the curve.

If one keeps in mind that the enclosed white spaces in the letters a, b, d, and q are oval in shape, he will be more likely to draw the hairlines flowing smoothly into the stems.

Fig. 27

66

Fig. 28

a d q

→ The red arrows indicate shallow joining of hairline to stem.

→ **Black arrows indicate the deeper joining.**

b h k m n u

h m n u

Fig. 29

On the hand lettering (top line) the stems have been adjusted to correct the illusion of the letters appearing to be wider at the open end.

h m n u

67

abcdefg

hijklmn

opqrstu

vwxyz

Plate 14

Caslon type italics

68

abcdefg
hijklmn
opqrstu
vwxyz

Plate 15

Hand-lettered Caslon italics

Simplified versions of the v, w, y, and z have been added to Plate 13. The decorative quality of these letters in the type forms —with the exception of the rather bizarre z—add interest to a line, but will make holes in a normally spaced caption. They should always be used when spacing allows, but the simplified forms will prove useful in getting even color in a tightly spaced line.

These italics should not have a sharp slant. Too great a slant on disconnected leaning letters will often damage their legibility.

As an aid in judging the relative proportions, note that the a, b, d, and q are identical in width at their widest point. The p is drawn a fraction narrower than these letters. The h, n, u, and simplified y are identical in width. The admitted white space in these letters should be optically as wide as the enclosed white spaces of the a, b, d, and q. The curves on the c and e are the same curves employed on the a and related letters. (Fig. 30).

Practice on the italic stroke-outs shown on Plate 16 should be done with a narrowed 2B sketching pencil. This exercise will be helpful in establishing the reason for the off-balance distribution of weights on the curved strokes, and for the sharp turns from the stems into the hairlines.

Stroking these letters out with a chiseled pencil can never truly reproduce the shape of the letter as it appears in finished form, but for layout purposes, only the general characteristics of the style are needed.

Fig. 30

abcdefg

hijklmn

opqrstu

vwxyz

Plate 16

zzyvw

71

Insurance
in child feeding
The New
GROWING TOGETHER

3 BILLION

PASSENGER MILES

TRIED &
PROVEN

Discovery

General Motors

HOW **NOT** TO DO IT

Displayed below are examples of errors which occurred most frequently in the drawing of Caslon letters. These copies of renderings by students were taken from an analysis of hundreds of completed problems. As these misinterpretations were made *after* a thorough description of the construction of each of the letters, it would indicate that they are the most difficult points of information to absorb, and are most likely to occur in the work of beginners. As a form of self-criticism, the reader should examine his own work to discover if these misdrawn letters appear in his caption. If so, he should restudy the draftsmanship of these letters shown on the Caslon Plate 13 and described on pages 64 to 67.

The lower curve of the belly has been drawn flat as it departs from the stem instead of the correct curving stroke.

Insufficient weight has been carried around the inside curve at the top of the stem making the curve appear too sharp.

Here the student failed to observe the proper shape of the enclosed white space. As a result the downstroke of the curve descends too sharply.

The greatest weight of the back curve has been placed too low on the curve and the upsweep turns up too sharply instead of following the true elipse of the letter.

The upsweep of the curve has been drawn wider than the eliptical form of the c, which can force the following letter away and cause a misspacing.

The hairline curving into the third stem has left the center stem at too high a point, causing an unpleasant shape in the admitted white space.

The upper joining stroke has been dipped too deeply into the stem which made it difficult to draw the proper widening of the curve at this point, and damaged the balance of the enclosed white space.

Too much weight has been carried around the curve, giving the curve the appearance of being heavier than the rigid stroke.

The curve departing from the left stem has been drawn much too flat.

74

The elipse is definitely off balance, with the top curve appearing too "square" and the bottom curve too sharp.

The letter is bottom-heavy because the maximum weight of the curve was placed much too low.

r

This letter contains two mistakes. The serifs are drawn too small for proper balance with the stem and the hairline stroke departing from the stem to form the kern is flat instead of curved.

The enclosed loop has been drawn too wide and deep, which causes it to dominate the upswept curve at the bottom.

s s

This misdrawing occurs all too often. The center stroke has been drawn in a straight line, instead of the gently curved shape.

The corners of the serifs were kept too far inside the horizontal guidelines, forcing the s into a "pothook" shape.

m

This student failed to gauge the width of the admitted white spaces, resulting in a badly placed center stem.

t

The triangular serif has been drawn too heavy in relationship to the weight of the vertical stroke.

The departure of the hairline curve into the kern was started too low on the left r and too high on the r at the right.

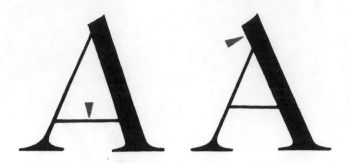

The student did not evaluate the balance of the enclosed white space to the admitted white space below and placed the hairline crossbar too low.

The weighted diagonal stroke has been allowed to travel too far above the meeting with the hairline diagonal.

The rigid stroke has been drawn too high, probably in a misguided effort to reduce the admitted white space.

The serifs have no optical relationship to each other, having been drawn in three different weights.

The top and bottom hairlines begin to curve too quickly, causing the letter to appear shorter than other letters in a line.

The lobe was dropped too deep, which overpowers the shortened tail.

Don't be a target for

winter ailments!

Art director's indication for trace-off practice.

A Statement

TO THE PUBLIC

Formal Scripts

The Formal Scripts, or round-hand letters, have been used in advertising layouts for many years. The classic beauty and legibility of these forms has kept them from becoming dated and I feel sure that they will continue to be of value, despite the everchanging trends in layout design.

These styles have an air of dignity and elegance which limits their use to layouts advertising products of a similar description. Their air of refinement is so obvious that we rarely see them misused.

Our present-day Formal Scripts are developments of early writings executed with a flexible pen. Today the lettering artist designs the letters on tracing tissue, transfers the caption onto his drawing paper, and builds up the letters with a pointed pen.

The quickest way to learn the "why" of the shapes of the basic strokes is to analyze the effects produced by the original tool. The shapes and the distribution of weights are the result of alternating light and heavy pressure on a flexible pen.

An analysis of the construction of the Formal Scripts will provide the proper background for subsequent studies of free-style scripts lettered with the pen or brush. Without this background, the beginner is all too likely to produce distorted and illegible free-styles.

LOWER CASE

The basic strokes shown in Fig. 31 are built-up examples which follow the design of the early writings. The beginner will be helped considerably by practicing the drawing of these strokes before attempting to letter a complete caption. Once the true forms of these strokes have been mastered, the most important step in the study of Formal Scripts has been taken.

Fig. 31

On examining Plate 17, note that the letters are drawn on a sharp slope. Most treatises on these scripts set the angle at 55°. However, moderate variations of the angle can be used without damaging the appearance of a caption.

The Formal Scripts should present a flowing, rhythmic line. *There must be no angular curves or angular joining of letters if this rhythm is to be maintained.* The hairline which connects the letters must flow *smoothly* into letters without a trace of an angle at the point of joining. The failure to observe this rule is common among students and some professional lettering men as well. Angular joinings destroy the rhythm of a line. (Fig. 32).

Fig. 32

a b c d e f g

h i j k l m n

o p q r s t u

v w x y z r

b f f p s x z r

Plate 17

81

The curve from the stem into the upswept hairline should form a leaning oval shape, with only enough weight carried around to insure a curved shape on the *inside* of the turn. Tommy Thompson, in his excellent book "The Script Letter," presents a logical method of insuring the correct amount of weight to be carried around the inside of a curved stroke. By imagining a small circle drawn inside the curve and placing only the amount of weight around the curve that the arc of the circle would allow, the weight will be properly controlled. This same effective method may be applied to the larger curved forms by envisioning a larger circle. (Fig. 33).

Fig. 33

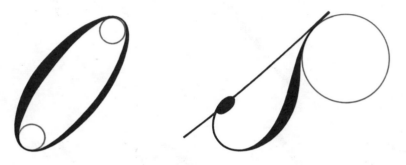

The widths of the upswept curves on all letters employing the shape must be alike, if good spacing is to be maintained. These letters are the a, d, h, i, k, l, m, n, p, t, u, and the alternate r. (Fig. 34).

Fig. 34

It is best to draw the outer line of the rigid diagonal lines and complete the hairline curves before the weight of the stroke is added. Draw the weighted line directly into the curve and then, imagining the small circle, add the slight carriage of weight around the turn. (Fig. 35).

Fig. 35

The hairlines which connect the letters, must join the letters at a high point. The maximum point of joining should be at half the height of the body of the letter. These joinings may be drawn below this point on a tightly spaced line, but should never go below one third the height of the letter. Once the point of joining has been established, it must be consistent throughout the line. (Fig. 36).

Fig. 36

On letters which are joined by a continuing hairline curving from the bottom of one letter to the top of the following letter, care must be taken to draw these in the same shape and width. Note that the connecting hairline is gently curved and is drawn on a slightly sharper diagonal than that of the rigid stems. (Fig. 37).

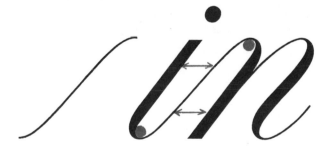

Fig. 37

The failure to maintain the similarity of the curves will place the hairline unevenly between the letters. On a tightly spaced line, the connecting hairline can follow the actual diagonal and be drawn fairly straight, but at no time should the hairline ever be drawn on a lesser angle than the established diagonal.

Letters are formed by the continuation of a basic stroke or by the combination of basic strokes. If the similarity of these strokes is maintained, the letters will be properly drawn and kept in correct relative proportion.

The basic stroke *C* when drawn with the flexible pen tends to increase in weight as pressure on the pen is applied on the downward stroke, placing the greatest width of the curve below the center. In reproducing this stroke by the build-up method, it is necessary to draw the outer edge of the curve on a slightly greater slope than the established diagonal, with the inner curve rounding gently along the true diagonal. This curve forms the lobes of the letters a, d, g, and q. It is also the major stroke of the c and e. Note however, that the upswept curve of the c and e is necessarily wider, to enable them to join the following letter without crowding. (Plate 18).

Some treatises on the Formal Scripts suggest that the o combined with a rigid diagonal line will aid the beginner in drawing the a, d, g, and q in identical shape and width. While this method is helpful in establishing the relationship of these letters, it will be noted on examining most renderings of the Formal Scripts, that the weight of the o is drawn in symmetrical balance while the weight of the lobes of the a, d, g, and q follow the *C* stroke. Also, the hairline which curves into the stem at the top of these letters does not dip as deeply into the stem as the actual joining of the letter o would produce.

The outside of the curved stroke
is drawn at a sharper angle than
the established diagonal.

The inside of the stroke forms a balanced arc
around the actual diagonal.

This places the greatest width
of the stroke below the center
of its height.

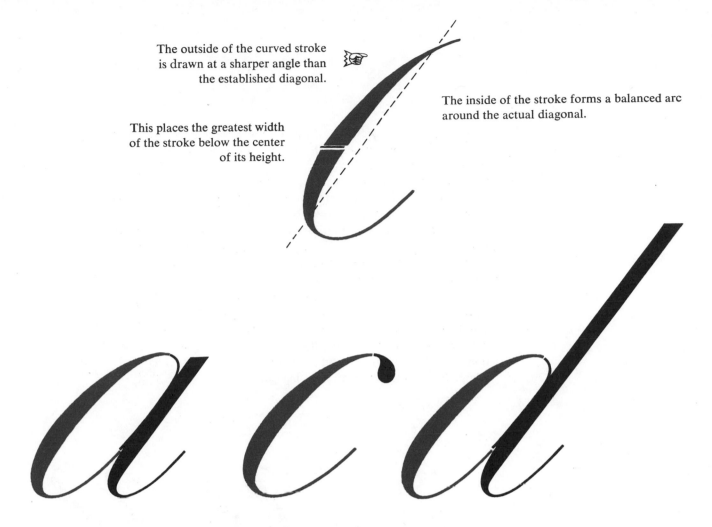

If the similarity of this basic stroke is maintained and properly joined to
the completing strokes, the letters will be in true relative proportion.

Plate 18

85

The basic stroke *l* when drawn with a flexible pen tends to produce a swelling stroke with its greatest width at the center of the stroke. This stroke forms a part of the h, m, n, p, u, v, and w, as shown on Plate 19. On the alternate r, shown on this plate, the upper curve is naturally not used. The tail of the k also follows the general form of this stroke in smaller size.

In most commercial captions the stroke is usually drawn with a moderate swelling, and in conservatively lettered captions, the weight is kept almost constant, with just a minor relaxing of the stroke to keep it from appearing rigid.

Due to the fact that these strokes curve away from the rigid stems at the bottom of the letter, they should be drawn on a slightly sharper diagonal to correct the illusion of the letter being wider at the open end. Care must be taken to avoid any exaggeration of this slight adjustment. Overdoing the angle of this stroke will produce an unpleasant "choking" of the letter. (Fig. 38).

Fig. 38

The letters shown in the Formal Script alphabet on Plate 17 are drawn in a fairly standard proportion and should be followed by the beginner before he attempts the more sophisticated renderings shown among the professional caption examples.

Present-day lettering artists often use variations of some of the original letter forms, shown in the alternate designs. Their use is entirely logical, as they fit in well with the basic Formal Scripts. As one learns more about the script letters, he will be able to note further departures from the original design in our contemporary scripts, than those shown here. These may be employed after he has mastered the basic forms. When any variations are used, however, they must be repeated consistently when they reappear in the same caption.

Plate 19

l

h *m* *m* *n*

This swelling stroke, drawn on a slightly sharper diagonal than the established diagonal, forms part of the letters below

p *n* *r* *u*

v *v* *w* *y*

The following rules governing the correct drawing of the Formal Scripts relate to the numbered arrows on Plate 20.

1 The hairlines joining the stems at the top of the a, d, g, and q do not dip deeply into the stems, but flow *smoothly* into the rigid lines. The lower hairlines meet the stem *high*. This will produce a balanced oval in the enclosed white space. (Fig. 40).

2 The hairlines on the h, k, m, n, p, and r depart from the stem at a low point to balance the high joining of the upswept hairlines. These hairlines *arc* away from the stems. They must never be drawn as straight lines.

3 The loop completing the e should be held above the center of the height of the letter. The enclosed white space should form a narrow, teardrop shape. (Fig. 39).

4 The hairlines on the descenders of the g, j, and y should be curved slightly as they travel upward to join the following letter, enabling a smooth joining. This curve also serves in keeping the hairlines from being drawn too close to the lower hairlines of the g and y.

5 When the alternate version of the r is employed, the hairline leaving the loop should not drop on a sharp angle. It may be drawn horizontally, or take a moderate downward angle. Too great an angle makes the letter appear optically smaller. The loop or point at the top must be sent above the horizontal line to maintain this optical balance. The loop should lean on the established diagonal.

6 The loop or point on the s must be sent above the line for the same reason. The weighted downsweep dips before rounding into its full curve as a counterbalance. Otherwise, the s would appear to lean on too sharp an angle. The graceful shape is held better if it is not connected to the following letter by a hairline.

7 The height and depth of ascenders and descenders must be kept in logical relationship to the body of the letters. Here, one's sense of design comes into play. I do not believe that any standard, relative proportions should be stated, as each caption will call for individual treatment. One should learn to judge whether these strokes are out of balance with the line.

a b c d e f g

h i j k l m n

o p q r s t u

v w x y z &

Plate 20

89

The problem of drawing the Formal Script letters in their relative proportions will be simplified if the similarity of the enclosed or admitted white space is kept in mind. The letters a, d, g, and q are identical in width as are the h, n, p, u, and y. (Figs. 40-41). The stems on the m are drawn closer together than those of the n to reduce the admitted white space. This same proportion of white space is also held on the v and w because of their hairline sides.

The general rules for spacing (page 11) should be followed, with the distance .between rigid diagonals establishing the widest space between the letters. You will note on examining the examples of Formal Script captions that the letters are drawn quite close together. *These scripts do not adapt well to wide letter spacing.* The b, o, v, and w which contain hairline sides

One can avoid drawing too overpowering an enclosed look on the e if the enclosed white space is held to a slim teardrop shape.

Fig. 39

If the narrow oval white space enclosed within the a, d, g, and q is held to a similar width, these letters will maintain their relationship of proportion.

Fig. 40

90

must be placed closer to the following letter than called for in the standard spacing rules. The c and e, being open-sided letters, should also be placed closer to the following letters.

Letters which are connected from bottom to top should be spaced at half again the distance between the rigid diagonal strokes. This connecting hairline does not hold sufficient weight to represent a character but must be considered as part of the general color of the line.

When working on the tracing tissues, diagonal guidelines should be drawn on each succeeding tissue and *traced through* onto the drawing paper to insure against any variation in the angle of the letters. The pencil should be kept sharp and the hairlines drawn as thin as they will be in inked form. The failure to do this will often result in a mis-spacing, as one is likely to misjudge the all over tone of a line if the hairlines are drawn with a blunt pencil.

Although many lettering men use a ruling pen and straightedge for executing the rigid lines, I believe that the beginner should draw these scripts free hand until his skill in pen handling is well developed. The inking of curved strokes will be made easier if the paper is turned as one follows around the curve. It is advisable to use a pen that will draw the weight of the hairline with a minimum of building up. Too fine a pen is likely to produce a "niggled" hairline or one too thin to hold through the reproduction process. It must be kept in mind that even a minor variation in the weight of the hairline will be a disrupting factor.

The whiting of the finished letters should be done with meticulous care. Formal Scripts should always be drawn with the sharp feeling of a steel engraving.

The admitted white space within the letters, h, n, p, u, and y should be identical in shape and volume.

Fig. 41

91

Duart makes women

American Hostess

A distinguished product

more beautiful

Constellation

THE *Beverly Hilton*

among food supplements

CAPITALS

The Formal Script capitals·offer considerable opportunity for expressing one's individual sense of design, but nonetheless, must contain certain basic strokes which are combined to produce a recognizable letter. Beginners, especially, are often tempted to design overly ornate capitals which conceal their identity among a mass of whirling strokes. There are occasions, of course, when very decorative letters can be used logically in advertising layouts, but they must always be readable. One should not attempt the more involved designs until he has learned to draw the letters in a fairly conservative form. When this has been accomplished, he is less likely to go overboard on the additional decoration.

The main strokes of the capitals are, like the lower cases, based on the effects produced by a flexible pen, used with varying pressure. These basic strokes are combined or extended into curving hairlines to produce all the letters in the alphabet.

In commercial captions, one will find various interpretations of the design of the basic strokes shown here, which, when logically used, produce pleasant variations of the conservative forms. These should be clipped and kept for future reference as an "inspirational" file, when the simpler forms have been mastered. (Though the term "inspirational" might be called "swipe" by some hard-bitten realists, it is not an uncommon practice to utilize good available examples when one has a limited time in which to produce his caption.)

Among the basic strokes presented are some which can be combined to produce a letter in two different forms, both of which are acceptable as Formal Script capitals. The examples shown here are the S, V, and W.

The body stroke, shown in red, appears in the greatest number of capital letters. It must be considered, then, as a most important stroke and drawn with great care. It should always appear to be optically parallel to the diagonal of the lower cases. Note that the shape swells equally on each side of the stroke, which places the maximum weight at its center.

The letters on the opposite page are produced by combining this body stroke with the basic strokes shown below in black.

B D F

H I J

K L

P R T

The stroke, shown in red, is essentially the same as the body stroke on the preceding page, but is drawn on a less acute angle in forming a major part of the V and W, combined with the basic strokes shown in black. Used as part of the M, N, and S, the angle is lessened even more.

The stroke shown above in red, combined with the additional strokes shown in black, produces the letters U and Y and the alternate renderings of the V and W. This stroke should lean a fraction more than the established diagonal, when it forms part of the U, W, and Y. This will prevent the illusion of a wider opening at the top of the letters when the strokes arc away from the rigid diagonals.

The oval stroke, shown in red, forms the major stroke of the C, O, and G.

Note that the weighted stroke of the A is the same stroke employed on the H and M.

The major stroke of the S is often swept outward in a greater curve, which actually produces a more recognizable letter. This departure from the established diagonal can be counterbalanced by the curving hairlines. The more direct S built by the continuation of the basic stroke into curving hairlines, is also compatible in a line of Formal Scripts.

As in the lower cases, the X is formed by combining an inverted C with an actual C.

The major stroke of the Q is also an inverted C combined with the horizontal swelling stroke.

The horizontal swelling stroke is used twice to produce the Z.

It is important to remember that the same basic strokes used in developing a series of letters must be drawn alike in shape and weight and held on the same diagonal.

The weight of the capitals must be held in ratio to their enlargement over the lower-case letters, at least. In most cases, the line will hold better color if the capitals are drawn actually heavier than the normal ratio would call for. However, regardless of the potency of the weighted strokes, the hairlines should be kept as thin as those on the lower cases. It should be noted that the curving hairlines occasionally pick up a bit of weight on a part of their arc. This is helpful in maintaining general color, but these weights should be kept secondary to the major weighted strokes.

Much care must be taken to avoid angular curves, which can pop out like a sore thumb, in the graceful capital forms. Once again, it will be helpful to examine the tissue upside down and from the reverse side in detecting these discrepancies.

An examination of commercial Formal Scripts shown on Plate 21 and in advertisements will show that, more often than not, the capital letters sweep below the base of the lower cases. This placement is not always necessary, but in many cases, will give better balance to the entire line.

Plate 21

102

Formal Script—capitals

D E F G

K L M

R S T

X Y Z

HOW **NOT** TO DO IT

Shown below are examples of the most frequently recurring errors made by students when working on this alphabet.

The top hairline has been dipped too deeply into the stem, destroying the balance of the oval white space.

Here, the basic stroke was ignored and the major weight of the curve was placed in the wrong position, above the optical center of the letter.

The enclosed loop has been stretched forward much too far, throwing the letter off the diagonal.

Two mistakes here. Too much weight was maintained at the top of the stem before rounding into the curve. The swelling stroke has been drawn on too sharp a diagonal which has caused a choking at the bottom of the letter.

This is the most common mistake allowing the hairlines to leave or join the stems too soon.

The loop of the r has been drawn off the diagonal and the hairline allowed to descend too rapidly.

The hairline leaving the loop was drawn straight instead of as a dipped form and the weight drawn too low on the curving stroke.

The balanced eliptical turn was ignored here and the curve drawn on an unpleasant sharp angle.

All the curves of this letter were drawn entirely too flat.

For a Lovelier Complexion!

This art director's rough was executed with a flat pencil for a quick effect. As the flat pencil does not reproduce the necessary swelling stroke, the student must not allow this indication to affect the true form of the letters.

THE BODONI LETTERS

THE BODONI LETTERS

The Bodoni letter forms can be classed among the earliest of the modern type faces. The great type designer, Giambattista Bodoni, departed from the humanistic forms generally used in the 18th century and produced letters of balanced weight and symmetrical curves. These letters were constructed from the standpoint of logical design, uninhibited by the influence of any tool upon their development. During his long and active life, Bodoni designed and cut scores of alphabets, many of which followed traditional forms. However, the examples shown in this chapter, represent the "modern" cuttings generally used in present-day advertising.

Until recent years, many type cuttings had degenerated from Bodoni's original forms, and one was more likely to find truer presentations of the Bodoni letters in well conceived hand lettering. The comparatively recent appearance of the Bauer Bodoni series, which follow Bodoni's original forms more closely, are a hopeful sign that a reconsideration of the fine Bodoni forms may become the trend.

Bodoni letters present a crisp, concise appearance, easily read in both caption and text form. Among their many logical uses, they are readily adaptable to the "contemporary" school of layout design because their simplicity of design makes them compatible to the general patterns of these formats. Bodoni can be employed in a wide range of weights without the resultant ugliness and loss of readability that occurs in many forms, such as weighted-up Caslons, Formal Scripts, Garamonds, and other alphabets of the traditional school. Because of their balanced weights, the letters can be condensed or expanded without the distortions that will occur in many other forms.

As a lettering specialist, I feel that there are many type alphabets or individual type letters that can be improved upon by competent hand lettering. This is especially so in the case of Bodoni ultra-bold letters, which could be considerably improved in the present type forms. The lettering artist also has the advantage of being able to make variations on the shapes of the kerns, the widths of serifs, and employ other stylizations without departing radically from the original Bodoni forms.

The major distinguishing features of the Bodoni letters which the beginner should note immediately are:

1   Symmetrical curves.

2   Balanced distribution of weights on the weighted curves, which reach their greatest width at the center of their arc.

3   Thin hairlines.   (Fig. 42).

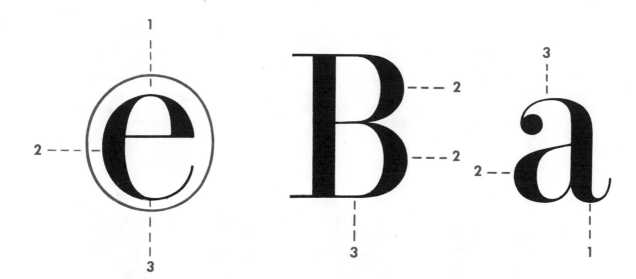

Fig. 42

It must also be noted that the carriage of weights around a curve is held to a minimum. Just enough weight should be carried to insure a smooth curve on the inside of the stroke. Any overcarriage of weight will reduce the amount of the single-weight hairline, which is one of the important factors in the Bodoni forms. (Fig. 43). In every Bodoni letter, capitals, lower case, and italics, regardless of weight or proportion, this single-weight hairline must be held around a section of any thinned, curving stroke.

Fig. 43

LOWER CASE

It is an interesting fact that Bodoni, among his numerous alphabets, never used the flat serif, now generally recognized as one of the characteristics of his letters. In every case, he designed these serifs in a swinging form, as shown in Fig. 44. Some of these curved hairline serifs were shallow enough to make the curve obscure in the smaller sizes, which may account for the misinterpretations that followed. The flat serif, accepted today as the true Bodoni serif, was designed by his contemporary, Didot. The Bauer Bodoni series has returned to the swinging serifs used in the original Bodoni lower cases and these will undoubtedly be used on future cuttings by other typographers. At the present time, a large majority of hand-lettered Bodoni used in advertising captions employs the flat Didot serif. (Fig. 45).

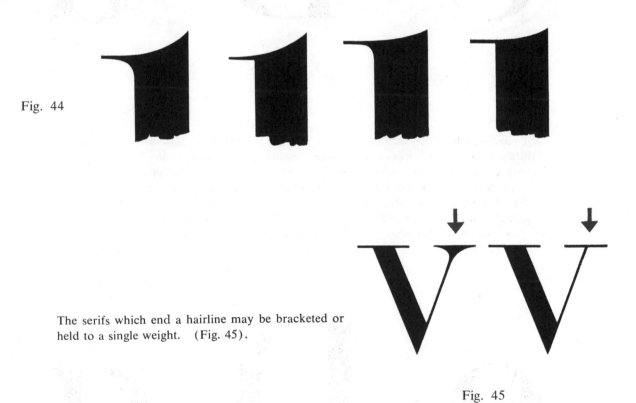

Fig. 44

The serifs which end a hairline may be bracketed or held to a single weight.   (Fig. 45).

Fig. 45

The example alphabets shown in this chapter employ the bracketed serif to end the hairline stroke, largely because they are more often used in advertising captions, but also, because they are helpful in holding more even color in a caption. However, there are times when the use of the unbracketed hairline serif can add sparkle to a caption when the copy or layout calls for this effect.

Fig. 46

In hand-lettered forms, one will find several variations in the shapes of the kerns. The circular kern is most often used and should be mastered by the beginner before attempting other variations. This kern is constructed by continuing the hairline as it arcs from the stem and rolling it into a tighter circle. If the kern is drawn as a true circle, this will allow white spaces to dip into the point of joining with the curving hairline.   (Fig. 46).

Some variations of this circular kern are shown below.   (Fig. 47). On occasion, the circular Kern is replaced by an oval form.

Fig. 47

Quicker
closing often
dictated by
tight
spacing

Exaggerated
sweep

Softened
joining of
hairline
to kern

Oval shape,
joining hairline
sharply

There are two choices in the joining of the curving hairlines to the stems on the lower case a, b, d, h, m, n, p, q, r, and u. These hairlines may flow smoothly into the stem, or the arc may be allowed to end as it meets the stem.   (Fig. 48).

Fig. 48

The upsweeping hairlines which complete the strokes on the a and t should always be kept in a balanced curve, regardless of tight letter-spacing, condensation, or expansion of these letters. These strokes are usually swung higher than on the type forms.   (Fig. 49).

In a tightly spaced line the hairline may run parallel to the stem after turning the curve.

Average sweep on letters of standard proportion.

Fig. 49

Wider sweep may be used on expanded letter in letter-spaced line.

112

An examination of many type examples of Bodoni will show that the inside of the curved strokes have been held quite flat, or with so minute an arc as to appear flat. While Bodoni did design alphabets which contained this design, the lettered expressions in use today almost invariably arc the inside of the curved stroke on letters of normal proportion.   (Fig. 50).

Fig. 50

a b c d e f
g h i j k l
m n o p q
r s t u v w
x y z

Plate 22

Bodoni type—lower case

a b c d e f
g h i j k l
m n o p q
r s t u v w
x y z ! ?

Plate 23

Hand-lettered Bodoni lower case

115

An example of the Bodoni lower-case type is shown for comparison with the hand-lettered alphabet on Plates 22 and 23.

The numbered arrows on the hand-lettered alphabet, point to the standard characteristics of the hand-lettered forms. While these refer to individual letters, the stated rules cover similar construction in other letters, as noted in the explanatory text.

1 The top arc of the a and the upswept hairline at the base of the stem are drawn as balanced arcs. Variations in the construction of the belly of the a are shown in Fig. 51.

2 The b shown here employs the flat serif, identified today with Bodoni. This has been held to on all other letters which contain flat serifs.

3 The balanced arc of the c produces the greatest weight of the curve at the exact center of its height. This balance is held on the letters b, c, d, e, o, p, q, and the small "o" used in the g.

4 The carriage of weight around the curve of the lobe of the d is held to the minimum needed to produce a pleasant inside curve. This applies to the letters named in paragraph 3 and also the inside curves on the a, h, m, n, and u.

5 The e provides a good example of the need to hold equal weight of hairline on all letters as this letter contains long strokes of the minimum hairline weight. Any variations of weight in these light strokes will be very obvious.

6 The curve from the stem of the h should be a balanced arc, which is repeated in the letters m, n, and u.

7 The hairline serif ending the hairline diagonal on the k may be bracketed, or held as a straight line. Whichever choice is made must be repeated on all serifs that end a hairline.

8 The hairline which curves away from the rigid stem of the n may depart from the stem at a higher point than on the type forms. This helps in holding the balanced arc of the curve. This point of departure is maintained on the h, m, n, r, and (in reverse) on the u.

9 The roll into the circular kern of the r is followed on the letters a, c, f, j, and y.

10 More weight is carried around the curves of the s than is used on present type forms. A variation of the standard serif is the use of a circular or oval kern, as on the italic s. The kern is more often used on bounced or relaxed versions of Bodoni lower cases. (Fig. 53).

11 Variations in the design of the top of the t are shown in Fig. 54. The upswept hairline on the t and a are swung higher than on the type forms.

12 The joining of the diagonals on the v and w should end with a sharp point. Because of this, these points should be sent a fraction more beyond the horizontal guidelines than the optical adjustment made for blunted points, as on the Caslon forms.

å b c d e f

g h i j k l

m n o p q

r s t u v w

x y z ! ?

Plate 24

117

Fig. 51

These shapes on the belly of the a are most generally used.

On ultra-bold letters and very condensed forms, the inside of the curved stroke is often held flat but this rigidity can be relieved by a minor carriage of weight into the hairline curve as opposed to the angularity of the type forms.

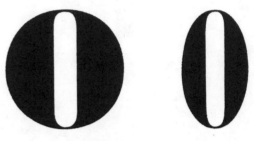

Fig. 52

This upright italic s, with rounded kerns often replaces the standard s in Bodoni captions.

Fig. 53

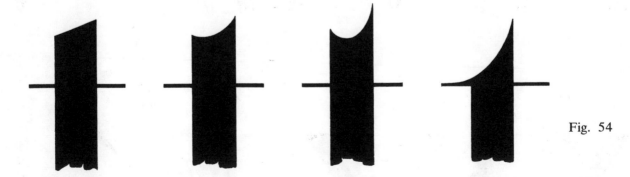

Fig. 54

Variations in the design of the top of the t.

The crispness of the formal Bodoni letters makes the use of a ruling pen logical for all the rigid lines. When the letters are bounced and relaxed in form, as shown in the professional examples, they should be done freehand. This becomes necessary in order to hold the casual effect of this kind of rendering.

Many alphabets lose considerable grace when they are weighted into bold or ultra-bold forms. This holds true to some extent with Bodoni, but if the symmetrical curves, balanced weights and thin hairlines are maintained, the letters will present a potent and readable caption.

Weighting these letters usually calls for flattening the inside of the curved strokes, but this rigidity can be relieved by a minor carriage of weight into the hairline curves, as opposed to the angularity of the type forms. Wherever possible, the horizontal serifs should be kept wide to provide a sufficient base for the bold strokes.

Flat endings, instead of points, are practical on the ultra-bold forms. (Fig. 55). The use of pointed endings will produce some distortion in the capital A, M, N, V, and W, and the lower case v and w.

Fig. 55

CAPITALS

Once the design of the lower-case forms is understood, drawing the Bodoni capitals should be relatively easy.

The same rules that control the shapes of the lower cases apply here and should be rechecked.

Therefore, the explanatory text following the numbered arrows on Plate 25, in many cases, contains some repetition of the description of the lower-case letters. The bracketed serifs employed here are more generally used in commercial captions. These changes described below should be checked against the type forms shown on Plate 26.

1 The meeting of the diagonal strokes of the A end in a sharp point, as on the M, N, V, and W. These sharp points should be sent further above and below the horizontal guideline than would be done with more blunted endings.

2 The curved strokes on the letters B, C, D, G, O, and Q are symmetrical curves, with the maximum weight placed at the center of the stroke.

3 The carriage of weight around the inside of all curves is held to a minimum in order to hold sufficient hairline. Just enough weight should be carried around to insure a pleasant inside curve.

4 The middle crossbar of the E is placed a fraction above the center of the height of the letter. This placement is followed on the letters B, F, H, and R.

5 The inside of the curved strokes maintains an arc, as against the flattened plane on the type forms.

6 The replacement of the curving upsweep to the horizontal serif on the type G, by a taller, vertical stroke is the most radical departure in the transition of the type to lettered forms. The G shown is generally used because it reduces the amount of white space admitted into the letter, which is helpful in letter-spacing.

7 The diagonals of the K may end in a point against the vertical stem or be drawn with the weighted diagonal departing from the hairline, clear of the stem. (Fig. 56).

8 The lobe of the P is drawn deeper than the lobes of the B and R, in order to reduce the white space admitted below the lobe.

9 The design of the tail of the type Q is rarely followed by lettering artists, who generally prefer some variations similar to the tail on the lettered Q.

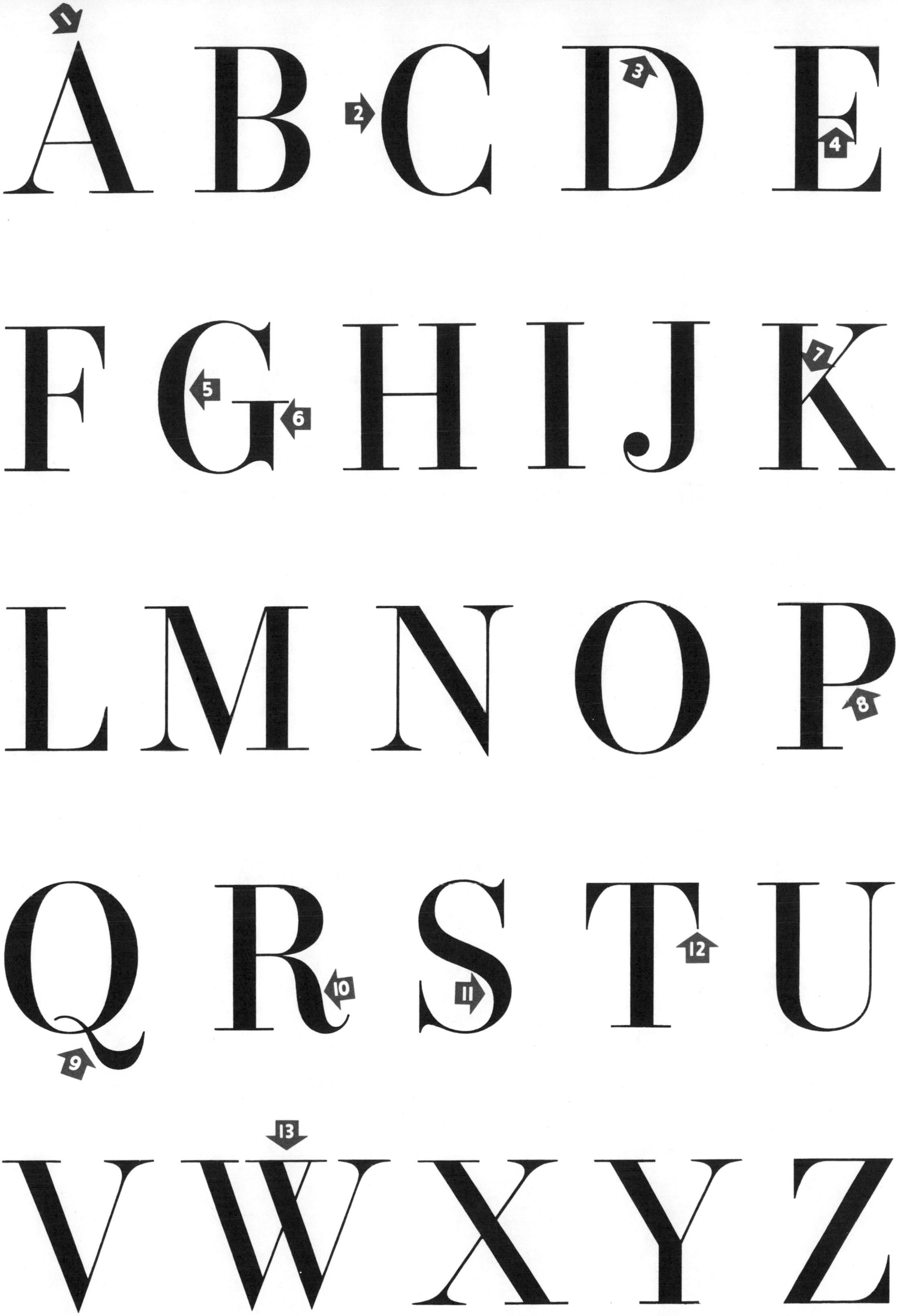
A B C D E
F G H I J K
L M N O P
Q R S T U
V W X Y Z
1
2
3
4
5
6
7
8
9
10
11
12
13

Plate 25

10 The tail of the R, often follows the type design, but is varied by swinging the hairline higher, or by drawing the tail vertically, a fraction forward of the lobe. (Fig. 56).

11 More weight is carried around the curves of the S than on the type forms.

12 The bracketed serifs of the T end in a fairly sharp point. This applies to the serifs on the C, E, F, G, and S.

13 The interlocked "V's" which form the W may be varied as shown on Fig. 56.

It should be noted that, as on all Roman capital forms, the necessity for optical balance calls for drawing the lower lobe of the B wider than the top lobe, the forward curve of the S a fraction forward of the top vertical serif and the X wider at its base.

Alternate designs of Bodoni capitals

K R W

Fig. 56

The diagonal lines meet the vertical stem with a point.

The tail of the R has been drawn vertically.

The inner hairline diagonal does not cross the weighted diagonal.

122

Low-Cost Luxury

REPORTS

ROYAL TRITON

DEPENDABLE

A B C D E
F G H I J K
L M N O P
Q R S T U

Plate 26
Bodoni type—capitals

V W X Y Z

124

A B C D E

F G H I J K

L M N O P

Q R S T U

Plate 27

Hand-lettered Bodoni capitals

V W X Y Z

ITALICS—LOWER CASE

A study of the hand-lettered interpretations of Bodoni lower-case italics will show a tendency among lettering artists to take more liberties with the standard design of the type forms, than is done in lettering the Roman forms. However, as on the preceding alphabet plates, the beginner is offered a conservative transition into the lettered forms as copy for his initial practice. As always, one is more likely to keep his personal interpretations of a letter within the realm of logic and good taste if he has first acquired a thorough understanding of the normal letter forms.

Even on conservative renderings, these italics are usually lettered narrower than the type proportions. Although they can be held on the same moderate diagonal of the type, they are most often drawn on a sharper slope. (Plate 28).

1 On examining the type alphabet, Plate 29, it should be noted that the distribution of weight on the curves of the a, b, c, d, e, o, p, and q does not follow the truly symmetrical balance found in the Romans. The greatest weights of the curves are placed a fraction below the center of the arc on the a, c, d, e, and q and a fraction above center on the b and p.

2 The only change in relative letter proportions are on the e, which is drawn narrower than the type proportion.

3 Both the type and hand-lettered alphabets carry a minimum amount of weight around the inside of the weighted curved strokes as they swing into the hairline strokes. The hand-lettered alphabet has been drawn to hold even more of the single-weight hairline around the curves of the h, m, n, and u.

4 On both alphabets, the swinging hairlines are swept high. Failure to do so will rob the letter of much of its grace. The flat, horizontal serifs used on the Roman forms are employed at the top of the lower-case stems.

5 The kerns may be drawn in either circular or oval shape, but must be consistent in their design in any one caption. In the lettered forms, one has the opportunity to draw a more graceful loop with the hairline, as it arcs toward the kern. This is on the f and j, because spacing is not affected by the more generous looping of the hairline above or below the body of the letters.

6 The capital Z form is usually employed as a lower case, replacing the ornate type z.

abcdef
ghijkl
mnopq
rstuvw
xyz

Plate 28

Hand-lettered Bodoni italics lower case

127

abcdef
ghijkl
mnopq
rstuvw
xyz

Plate 29

Bodoni type italics—lower case

abcdef
ghijkl
mnopq
rstuvw
xyz

129

In recent years, many lettered captions have included some radical departures from the standard Bodoni italic letters.

The change most regularly used—the replacement of the type y, with the simplified lettered y, which is drawn by adding a descender to the u shape—is obviously helpful from the standpoint of spacing. The same holds true in the change often made on the lettered g, which is formed by adding a descender to the a.

The Roman a and e—and occasionally, the y, v, and w—are being used as italics. Although these are radical changes, their inclusion in a caption can give the line a different and interesting effect.

The type k is often lettered in the form shown on the following page.

Lettering artists allow themselves the choice of using horizontal serifs on the v, w, and simplified y, in place of the curving hairlines.

The flat serif is sometimes repeated on the right hand stem of the u and simplified y.

Bodoni lower-case italics are often lettered with the same definite off-balance distribution of weights on curving strokes, which appear in the Caslon italics and other humanistic alphabets. By retaining the horizontal serifs and thin, single-weight hairlines, this interpretation maintains a Bodoni "feel" and combines well with the standard Bodoni Romans. However, they have been properly called "Casdoni" because the letters are actually a combination of both styles.

a e g

k v y

America's Finest

Lockheed technicians are on the job

FORD

Folks everywhere...

cook 'em with

WHEN YOUR DOORBELL RINGS

DOORBELL RINGS

Split-second starts

The Bryson Lectures

HOW <u>NOT</u> TO DO IT

Shown below are examples of the most frequently recurring errors made by students when working on this alphabet.

The top arc has not been held on a symmetrical curve, thus destroying the Bodoni characteristic.

Far too much weight has been sent around the inside of the curves. This is a cardinal sin in drawing the Bodoni letters.

The kern was not drawn in optical relationship to the weight of the letter, and appears too insignificant.

The curving hairline has been allowed to widen too rapidly, rather than holding to a single weight until it nears the downstroke.

The bottom arc was not drawn on the same ellipse as the curve on the top, which crippled the symmetry of the lobe.

Here the student failed to note that the weight of the center stroke should diminish as it rounds a curve.

The top of the letter was drawn too narrow for correct balance with the vertical stroke.

The horizontal serif is placed too low, allowing too much admission of white space.

The "V" stroke within the letter has not been centered between the vertical strokes.

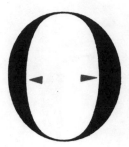

Although the sharp points on the Bodoni letters are usually sent a fraction more above and below the horizontal guidelines than is done with letters containing blunted points, there is often a tendency to overdo this optical correction, as has been done on this N.

The student failed to judge the sameness of weights on the curved sides.

The lobe was drawn too deep which damaged the proportion of the letters.

The lobe was drawn wider than the tail of the R, throwing the letter off balance.

Are you hearing only a FRACTION of PIAZZA'S voice?

MAGNAVOX

137

Brush Scripts

and

Brush Letters

Brush Scripts

and

Brush Letters

The use of free-style brush scripts and brush letters in advertising layouts began to gain momentum about twenty-five years ago. Preceding this period, conservative scripts, with a semblance of brush quality, had been used, but the more free renderings of the present were avoided because most advertising men at that time felt that they were not easy to read.

The placement of advertisements, done in continuity cartoon format, in the comic supplements of Sunday newspapers, helped considerably in increasing the use of brush scripts and brush letters. Because we are a nation of inveterate comic-strip readers, research proved that these advertisements held a high readership rating. In order to present the same physical appearance of an actual "comic" and thus draw the reader's eye into the advertisement under the impression that he was being introduced to a new strip, the use of formal captions was naturally excluded. The title panels called for styles which would be compatible to the cartoon feeling of the advertisement. The brush letters used were merely blown-up renderings of the copy in the cartoon "balloons" and the brush scripts employed were more readable copies of the bulbous title scripts of that time. Currently, cartoon titles are done in many styles and the comic supplement advertisements themselves have evolved into more obvious advertisements, but during this transition the brush scripts and letters began to be widely used in magazine and newspaper layouts.

Any research into the popular "runs" of a particular letter style will show a pattern of heavy usage over a period of time, followed by a definite slackening, as another style becomes the current favorite. The good basic alphabets, proven sound by long-time use, often reappear as a cycle is completed, despite the developments of newer type and lettering styles.

In the case of the brush scripts and letters, their "run" was phenomenal, as they grew in popularity year after year, until, about two years before this writing, a large majority of advertisements employed varying expressions of these styles for captions and subcaptions. This overuse tended to defeat the purpose of these styles, which was to achieve a "different" effect.

At this point, many art directors began to realize that the saturation point had been reached and a swing to other styles was necessary in order to regain the "different effect". The use of the brush scripts and letters in current advertising has been reduced considerably, which once again makes them an effective style to use when they can add to the flavor of the layout. I am sure that these styles will be employed for many years to come, if held in proper ratio to the pattern of advertising captions.

Widely differing effects can be produced by the brush, depending upon the weight and technique employed. Light executions can add an air of quality, light-heartedness, speed, etc. On the other extreme of weights, ultra-bold letters give the impression of strength, shock, drama, and impact. The effects produced by the intermediate weights, depend largely upon the style used and the texture of the edges of the letters. In many cases, a dry-brush technique will add to the attention value of the caption. Pages 162 and 163 show examples of various styles which properly interpret the mood of the statement.

There are occasions when the best format for selling a specific product will call for square or rectangular shapes. Brush letters are helpful in this conservative format. In many cases, as in the General Electric layout shown, an effective use of brush lettering is made by combining a word or two of these styles with a conservative type form.

The word "hurricane" has been lettered to express the necessary feeling of excitement.

SECTION **1**

EXECUTION of the BRUSH SCRIPTS

As a general rule, a beginner will find the free renderings of brush scripts more difficult than that of the formal styles. There are no standard rules to serve as a control, but ability will develop with patient practice until one learns what the brush can produce for him. *The one rule that must be remembered is that the words must be easily read and yet present a spontaneous effect.*

In beginning this study, the student must constantly guard against his own handwriting influencing the shapes of the brushscript letters. Most people have some individual characteristics in their handwriting which can inhibit the execution of differing brush styles, unless they keep on the alert to prevent these personal characteristics from setting up a standard and repetitious way of brushing out any particular letter.

I've had several beginning students tell me that they felt sure that they could not execute a readable brush script because their handwriting was "awful". That is a misconception that must be cleared at the start. One's own handwriting should be forgotten in this study—if not, it will be impossible to produce variations in the shapes of the letters. What's more, the majority of script captions *would* be awful, as the average artist is not noted for the legibility of his handwriting. While there can be some debate as to whether brush scripts fall into the actual lettering classification, they can safely be described as a form of *controlled* writing. Habit patterns should be consciously avoided. One must begin to experiment with various ways of writing the same letter from the start.   (Fig. 57).

Fig. 57

Professionally, brush script and brush letter captions are achieved by several methods. The best approach for the beginner—and the method most commonly used professionally—is the spontaneous write-out of the established copy many times. No guidelines should be used unless one has difficulty in holding his line in a reasonably horizontal position, in which case a single horizontal line should be used with the letters written above and below the line. (Fig. 58). The use of guidelines is too likely to restrain the bounce of the letters.

Control of horizontal

Fig. 58

The write-outs should then be examined for words or even parts of words which have produced the desired effect and style. If these segments are related in weight and angle, they can then be pasted into a complete caption and carefully retouched with lampblack or ink, and white paint. The joining of assembled parts of words must be completed and all necessary retouching done on the letters.

The professional rarely delivers his brush captions to the art director in this paste-up form. The assembled caption is sent to be photostated for a negative print. The cut marks are then painted out on the negative, after which the caption can be examined carefully for any additional retouching of the letters with lampblack and white paint. A glossy positive print—which can be reproduced more sharply than a mat print by the photoengraver—is then made and delivered to the art director as the finished work. Even though art directors are aware of this paste-up approach to a brush caption, the photostat still gives the impression of the caption having been written out in its entirety, just as easy as pie!

You can't help but succeed !

You can't help but succeed !

You can't help but succeed

succeed !

The beginner will have to write out many more lines
of a sentence than those shown on this page before
he can hope to find enough words or parts of words
which can be assembled into a complete caption.

succeed !

can't help

The cutout segments are cemented down on heavier board and retouched.

Further retouching can be done on the negative.

You can't help but succeed!

The positive print is then considered to be the finished art.

You can't help but succeed!

Examples of the development of Brush captions by Herman Spinadel.

You can't help but succeed!

You can't help but succeed!

The beginner will have to write out many more lines
of a sentence than those shown on this page before
he can hope to find enough words or parts of words
which can be assembled into a complete caption.

You can't help but succeed!

succeed

You

help

can't

146

The cutout segments are cemented down on heavier board and retouched.

Further retouching can be done on the negative.

You can't help but succeed!

The positive print is then considered to be the finished art.

You can't help but succeed!

At the beginning, I believe that a student should not try to work for a specific expression of the brush script, and should start his practice without any professional clippings in front of him. Much of the spontaneous quality will be lost if one tries painstakingly to copy another man's rendering at this stage.

I recommend a solution of lampblack be used for the initial practice, mixed in a container to a consistency that will flow freely from the brush and yet produce a dark stroke. Ink may be used, of course, but it does shorten the life of a brush. As a lot of practice is necessary before one can loosen up sufficiently to get a spontaneous effect, it will be economical to practice on newspaper pages. When good results begin to show, one should decide on the copy he wants to write out and switch to bond paper, which can be easily cut and reassembled on heavier stock.

I have found that writing a slanted script of medium weight comes more naturally to most beginners and suggest that the practice begin with this style. A #2 brush will be best for the medium weights. Actually, a fairly small brush such as the #2 or #3 will produce any desired weight, depending on how the brush is held and how much pressure is applied.

However, each lettering artist will decide in time, just what size brushes work best for him. Many professional letterers "barber" their brushes to various angles to get certain effects, and some prefer long-haired rigger brushes. Choosing the right type of brush, as experience is gained, becomes a purely personal decision, but at the start a fairly worn brush or a new one with the fine hairs cut from the point will serve the purpose.

The speed with which one writes out the letters is also a matter of individual decision. Some may get the best results by very fast brushing, while others may tend to produce illegible letters by working too fast. Continued experimentation will help to establish the best speed of execution for each individual. However, working too slowly will almost inevitably produce a labored and uninteresting line.

Light stroke. For the light letters the brush should be spun into a point to remove surplus solution. It should be held almost vertically and only the point of the brush allowed to touch the paper.

Medium stroke. Drawing intermediate weights calls for holding the brush on a moderate angle which will produce a wider stroke that will maintain a fairly constant weight. The angled brush will also prevent the stroke from starting with a point and swelling in weight as the stroke is continued . . . a bulbous shape that will detract from the readability of the caption.

Heavy stroke. The brush should be well loaded with the lampblack solution. It should be held on a sharp angle and definite pressure should be applied on the stroking.

The amount of bounce and variation in the height of the letters in a brush script caption depends upon the needs of the layout and is usually decided upon by the art director. Brush scripts can range from a conservative rendering to a highly excited version. In almost all cases it is advisable to vary the size of the letters to some degree to prevent a static presentation. Care must be taken to keep the words from enlarging or diminishing steadily, or forming an arc caused by enlarging the letters in the middle of a word. (Fig. 59).

Fig. 59

The original exercise should include: a leaning, medium-weight line; an upright medium weight; a very light leaning line; and an upright ultra-bold line. The letters should be drawn fairly large at the start, roughly from ¾ of an inch to 1 inch high. The strokes should be made using the forearm and resting the heel of the hand on the paper, lightly, with no movement of the fingers.

In many cases, one often finds that one word or more has not been satisfactorily written to complete the line. When this happens it should be rewritten with the rest of the line in front of you to serve as the control for average height, weight, and angle. Long words which give trouble in execution can often be broken at a logical spot to allow the reloaded brush to get a fresh start. This will also serve in holding the general weight of the letters.

Rubber cement should be used for paste-up assembly. The paper on which the assembly is to be made, and the cut out pieces, should be coated and allowed to dry. Then the pieces should be recoated and placed down wet, so that they can be slid easily into their correct positions. Because the brush script words are connected units, the words should be placed quite close together, otherwise the line will tend to fall apart.

It is only when the beginner has assembled several differing lines, done without attempting to copy specific styles, that this exercise begins to "pay off". Now is the time to compare these captions with professional examples shown in this chapter and with other clippings which he should collect for reference. In many cases he will find that his brush has produced letters or words similar to the professional renderings. This should enable him to analyze the results of correct brush handling much more objectively than if he had studied the professional examples "cold". He should be able to spot his misdrawn letters more easily.

It is important to note that when the brush rounds the curve at the bottom of the rounded letters, it tends to produce a flattened arc on the outside of the curve, while the inside white space comes to either a blunted or sharp point. If the brush is held properly, this will occur naturally and will prevent any "blobbiness" at the turning point. (Fig. 60).

The student should retouch his captions with lampblack and white paint, joining the disconnected segments where necessary, removing unnecessary brush flicks and restoring illegible letters, all the while examining similar letters in his professional examples.

It should be understood that this write-out, cut-and-paste approach is only one of the methods employed in the field, but it is the quickest road to the understanding of these styles. Many lettering artists use the original stroke-outs as underlays only, and *build* up the words on a sheet of transparent or translucent paper, using as few strokes as possible, correcting as they go, yet trying to hold the spontaneous feel of the caption. Sometimes, these are run through many times before he is satisfied with the results. The build-up cannot be done effectively by using slow, niggly strokes, but with strokes which, though controlled, develop the letters quickly. Another approach used by men who know just what the brush *should* produce, is that of laying in the line with a blunt charcoal or carbon pencil, and using it for an underlay for the brush rendering.

Fig. 60

SECTION **2**

BRUSH LETTERS

The brush letters present a somewhat different problem than the scripts. If they are drawn spontaneously, using the stroke-out method, one does not have the advantage of gaining the "happy accidents" that may occur in the continuous stroking of a script word. The disconnected letters call for more forethought in planning the shapes. One must mentally preplan the stroke he wants, place the tip of the brush to the paper—holding it at an angle that will produce both a flattened top and the desired weight—and draw the stroke with enough speed to avoid a wobbly line.

Although many brush letter captions are developed by using the cut-and-paste method after several captions have been stroked out, the majority of the commercial captions appearing today are the results of quick build-ups, worked over a series of underlays. A heavy vellum paper is best for this method of development. The conservative capital and lower-case alphabets shown on pages 154 and 155 should be followed by the beginner before attempting more freely rendered forms.

The starting practice should be done by the direct stroke-out and assembly. These assembled captions will then be helpful as underlays in experimenting with the quick build-ups.

It is extremely important to remember that brush letters must *not* be letter spaced. They are always held close together and in many places, can touch one another when the connections do not hinder their readability.

On examining the commercial captions shown on page 163 and the alphabet plates, it must be noted that both the vertical and slanted forms never use a stem stroke that bows against the forward movement of the line but are held as straight lines or curved slightly forward. Also note that the horizontal strokes do not arc sharply upward but are drawn straight, or angled slightly upward, or drawn in a minor arc which curves along the horizontal.   (Fig. 61).

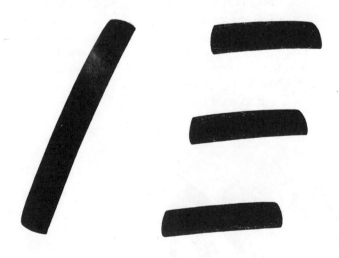

Fig. 61

The proper execution of these strokes will hold the feeling of speed in letters such as shown in Fig. 62. The tendency to reverse these strokes is very common among beginners.

Fig. 62

On letters constructed with, or containing diagonals, the arced line may be combined with a straight stroke. (Fig. 63). These rules also apply to the similar strokes on the lower-case letters.

Fig. 63

abcdef
ghijkl
mnopq
rstuvw

Plate 31 – Lower-case Brush letters (above) and capitals (opposite).

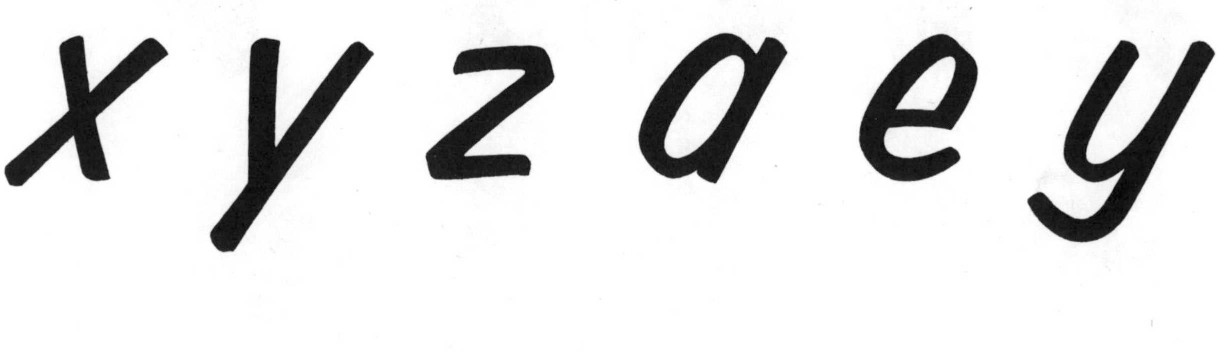

xyzaey

154

A B C D E

F G H I J K

L M N O P

Q R S T U

V W X Y Z

The cutout segments are cemented down on heavier board and retouched.

Further retouching can be done on the negative.

the most important decision

The positive print is then considered to be the finished art.

the most important decision

Examples of the development of Brush captions by Herman Spinadel.

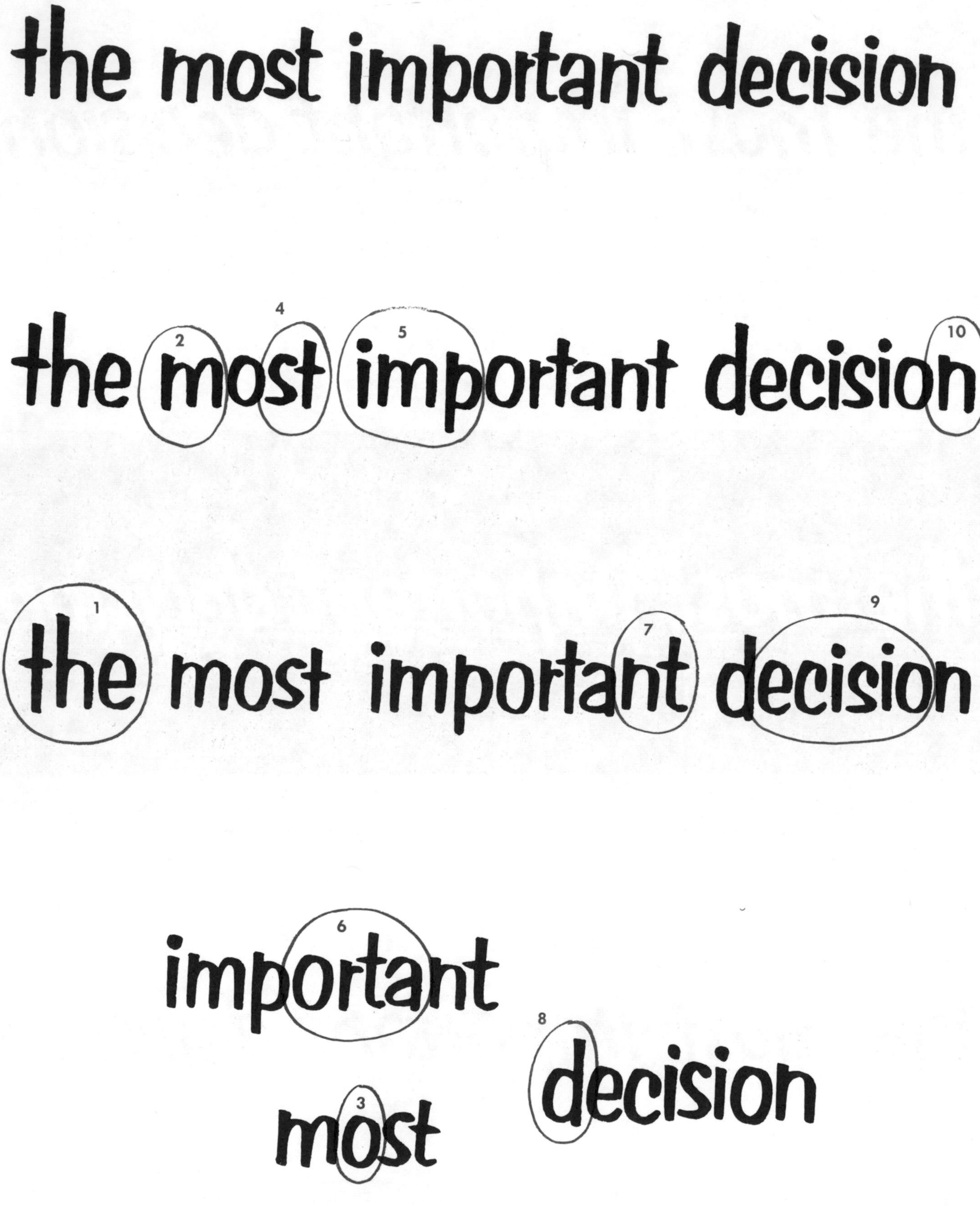

the most important decision

the most important decision

the most important decision

important

most

decision

The cutout segments are cemented down on heavier board and retouched.

Further retouching can be done on the negative.

the most important decision

The positive print is then considered to be the finished art.

the most important decision

On a spontaneous write-out of the brush letters, one must remember that most of the letters should not be drawn with a continuous stroke, but by a combination of strokes.   (Fig. 64).

Fig. 64

V X Z

The reader will note that on some of the examples shown, the strokes tend to diminish as they travel downward. These strokes are logical, as well as strokes that hold a consistent weight, but one should studiously avoid allowing a stroke to widen as it descends, as this will produce an unpleasant, bottom-heavy line.

These initial workouts in the brush scripts and brush letters will rarely produce a commercially acceptable caption, but they have much value in developing the observation and sense of discrimination for the beginner. He can then begin to experiment in developing his own interpretation of the brush forms, based on what he has learned about the actions of a brush. Working with a style which has no background of historical development, and controlled only by the need to develop a spontaneous and legible caption, the field is wide open for new expressions.

HOP TO IT!
SAVE 10¢

The Orchid Isle

The Garden Isle

To *him*
you're just as lovely
as a movie star

the slender figure

Instant Chase & Sanborn "Tear Out" Coupon!
This <u>really</u> is <u>real</u> coffee!

YOU CAN GET THE WHITEST, BRIGHTEST WASH WITH THE NEW G-E ACTIVATOR-AUTOMATIC

Taste why new Swans Down Mix wins over all other leading cake mixes!

Today's fashion —

HOW <u>NOT</u> TO DO IT

Shown below are examples of the most frequently recurring errors made by students when working on this alphabet.

The belly of the a has left the stem too high, dominating the entire letter.

This e is a hybrid, containing neither the curved loop nor the horizontal crossbar.

The arc at the top of this a is too skimpy throwing the letter off balance.

Here, the short stem should have followed the diagonal of the ascending stroke.

The upsweep at the bottom has not been swung forward or upward far enough making the letter lean on a sharper diagonal.

The enclosed loop of the e has been drawn too tight leaving only a sliver of enclosed white space which might bleed shut when reproduced.

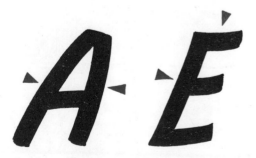

The natural forward arc that forms these letters has been ignored, resulting in static and unpleasant forms.

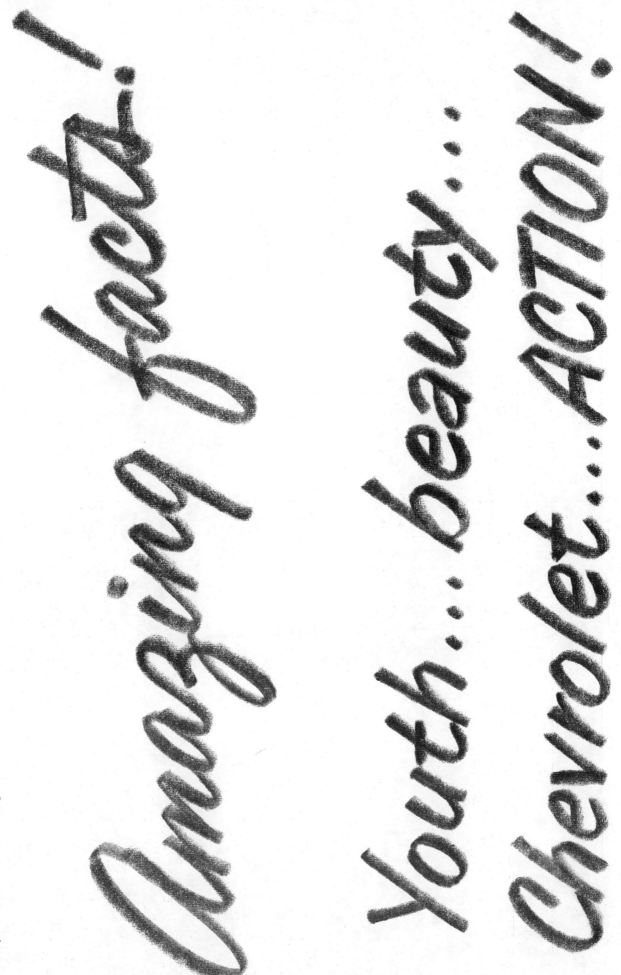

Amazing facts!

Youth....beauty....

Chevrolet....ACTION!

THE GOTHIC LETTERS

Block letters first appeared in England at the beginning of the 19th century. They were originally called "Egyptian" and are now known in Europe as "Grotesque", or by the general term "Sans-serif". In the United States they have been misnamed "Gothics" and although that name is illogical for these forms, long-time usage has made it the generally accepted term.

There are literally scores of alphabets which fall into the Gothic classification. The majority of these are single weight, sans-serif letters. The exceptions are letters containing a minor variation in the weight of the strokes, as found in Franklin Gothics. In many cases, differently named Gothic forms are only slightly dissimilar in design.

These forms are widely used in advertisements. Being easily read, they are also the most commonly used letters on outdoor posters. The weights may range from hairlines to ultra-bold, which makes them adaptable to a large variety of layout designs.

When hand lettered, the Gothics are extremely elastic and may be drawn in narrowly condensed, or widely expanded forms without the appearance of distortion produced in letters of less simple design. When light faces are called for, the message is delivered clearly without overpowering other elements in the layout. The bold faces provide the impact called for on "heavy selling" advertisements. However, the use of ultra-bold faces is often overdone, due to the mistaken impression that their powerful impact will attract more attention. Actually, the overuse of ultra-bold letters hampers their readability.

GOTHIC

FLAT SIDED FORMS

At first glance, Gothic letters seem easy to draw. The characters appear to be of uniform weight and to present no problem other than that of careful measurement. Actually, several adjustments in the weights must be made to produce the even color that these letters present to the eye. Without these adjustments, which produce an *optical* evenness of weight, a Gothic caption will lose much of its quality and readability. Discrepancies in the optical similarity of the weights, and in proportion and spacing, are more obvious in a Gothic caption than in captions employing letters which contain hairlines and serifs.

The flat-sided letters, such as Alternate Gothic and condensed News Gothic serve a definite purpose in the advertising field. They were designed specifically to admit a maximum number of characters into a given width without loss of height or readability. They are completely familiar to the general public because of their common usage for newspaper headlines. In fact, they are often employed by art directors to give the impression that the advertising caption *is* a news headline.

The lettering artist has considerable opportunity to improve upon many of the Gothic type forms. In some rare cases, the type has been so well designed that only minimum changes are advisable. However, since there are numerous occasions when these forms must be lettered, such as on posters, and in cases when the weight and proportions of the type will not fit the layout, the experienced lettering man may justifiably contribute his own interpretation of the type.

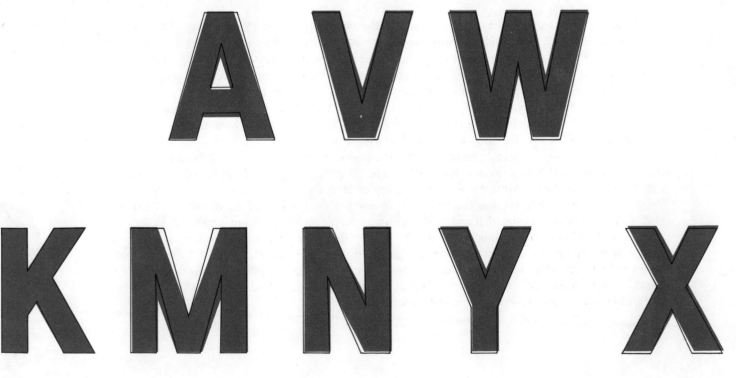

Fig. 65

The red arrows on Plate 32 indicate the adjustments that can be made on the flat-sided letters.

The major pitfall to be avoided in lettering Gothics is the massing of color which will result from the incorrect drawing of letters containing diagonal lines. The letters in this group are A, K, M, N, V, W, X, and Y. This massing of color occurs when the diagonal lines join each other, as on the A, V, and W; when the diagonal lines meet the vertical stems on the K, M, N, and Y, and in the crossed diagonals of the X. Some additional weight at these points is unavoidable, but it can and should be reduced.

Fig. 65 shows the maximum massing of weight that will occur if the letters were to be drawn with all the strokes exactly the same weight. The lines on this example are traced from Fig. 66 which shows the letters drawn with optically adjusted lines.

On the A, N, and V, the top or base of the letter is drawn *wider* than the width of the stems, where the diagonals join each other or join the vertical stems. This widening is made necessary by the fact that the white space must be forced as deeply into the color mass as it can logically go without obvious distortion. The weights of the diagonal lines diminish slightly on the *inside* as they travel toward the joining point, sending the wedge of white space a fraction deeper into the color mass. Many lettering artists carry this a step further by forcing an additional point of white paint into the angle. I feel that this last correction should be restricted to lettering which is to be reproduced in newspapers or on other soft papers as a protection against ink bleed.

On the M and W, only the outer joinings of the diagonals are widened at their meeting point. The vertical stems on the M and the outer diagonals of the W diminish slightly in weight on the *inside* as they travel toward the joining point. The inner diagonals must be drawn *narrower* than all other diagonal lines in the alphabet as the greatest bulking of weight appears in these letters. These thinner diagonals produce no color mass when they meet and need no adjustment. Their point of joining need be no wider than the width of the stems.

The short diagonals on the K and Y diminish slightly in weight on the *inside* as they approach the vertical stems.

The crossed diagonal lines of the X diminish slightly in weight on the *inside* as they travel toward the point of crossing.

The diagonal line of the Z needs no reduction in weight and has parallel sides.

Keep in mind that all lines which diminish in weight must appear optically to have parallel sides. The diminishing should never be obvious.

Fig. 66

1. The horizontal plane, where the diagonals meet, has been drawn wider than the width of the stems and the lines diminish in weight as described in detail on the preceding pages.

2. The diagonal lines of the M, N, Z, and the inner diagonals of the W have *parallel* sides. The color reduction on the M, N, and Z is made by the diminishing weights of the outer strokes combined with the thinner diagonals. The diagonal of the Z calls for thinning in the bolder faces only, because of an optical illusion that weighted diagonal lines appear to be wider than a vertical line of the same width.

3. All horizontal lines on single-weight Gothics should be drawn a fraction thinner than the width of the vertical lines. This adjustment is made because horizontal lines equal in width to vertical lines appear optically heavier. (Fig. 67).

4. The thickness of the semi-circular curves at the top and bottom of the letters C, G, O, Q, S, and U should be slightly thinner than the width of the vertical stems to hold an optical relationship of weight. (Fig. 68). As in the case of the horizontal lines, this reduction of weight must be minor, avoiding the appearance of a perceptibly thinned line.

5. The center crossbars of the B, R, E, and H are drawn a fraction above the center of the letters to produce a better balance of white space.

6. The lower crossbar of the F and P may be drawn lower to reduce the admitted white space between letters.

7. The crossbar of the A is necessarily well below the center. Its placement is governed by a balanced relationship between the enclosed white space and the admitted white space below the crossbar.

8. The curve of the lobes on the B, D, P, and R should follow the arc of a small circle. These are often misdrawn with either too sharp or too soft a turn. (Fig. 69). The inside of the curve should appear to run parallel to the outer curve. If the inside curve is too soft, the strokes will tend to weight up around the curves. Note that the properly drawn turns tend to allow a sufficient dip-in of white space into the middle crossbar of the B and R.

9. The strokes which complete the curves on the C, G, and S should be drawn fairly long in order to reduce the admitted white space. When these strokes are too short, as on several type faces, the volume of white space will produce holes in the line. (Fig. 70).

10. The tail of the R may be flicked forward at the bottom or held with sharp corners. This minor point of design is often overdone by bending the entire stem.

11. The S is often lettered with curved sides, but can be more easily spaced when the sides are kept flat. This should also be done on the lobes of the B, P, and R.

ÅBCDEF

GHIJKL

MNOPQR

STUVWX

YZ?

Plate 32

Hand-lettered flat-sided Gothic capitals

171

It must be thoroughly understood that the adjustments to produce optical evenness of weight should be made with restraint. An over-doctored letter is as bad as an uncorrected one.

Any given mathematical measurement of the reductions in weight would be too minute to be of value to the beginner. The development of one's sense of observation is the major factor in achieving the correct optical weights.

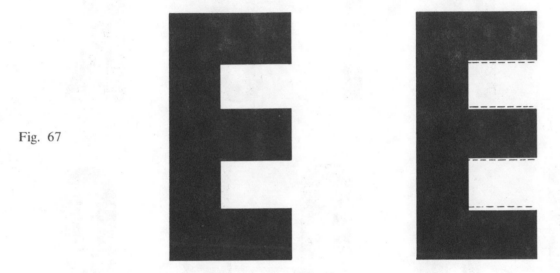

Fig. 67

All horizontal lines on single-weight Gothics should be drawn a fraction thinner than the width of the vertical lines.

The semicircular curves at the top and bottom of these letters should be slightly thinner than the width of the vertical stems.

Black lines indicate width of vertical lines.
The weight around the curves has been slightly reduced.

Fig. 68

Fig. 69

The curve of the lobes on the B, D, P, and R should be carefully drawn to avoid making them too sharp or too soft.

The strokes which complete the curves on the C, G, and S should be drawn fairly long in order to reduce the admitted white space.

Fig. 70

A B C D E F

G H I J K L

M N O P Q R

S T U V W X

Y Z

Plate 33

Alternate Gothic No. 1 type

174

A B C D E F

G H I J K L

M N O P Q R

S T U V W X

Y Z ?

Plate 34

Hand-lettered flat-sided Gothic capitals

A ruling pen and straightedge should be used in the inking of the formal Gothic letters. However, all curves should be drawn freehand rather than with a compass. The compass produces the illusion of a slight "point" at the outer center of the curves. Although the curves appear to be truly semi-circular, a fraction more "shoulder" should be drawn on the sides of the curve to produce this effect. The curves must flow smoothly into the rigid stems without producing a "corner".   (Fig. 71).

To insure that the turns on the lobes of the B, D, P, and R will not be drawn too heavy, the inside curve should not be added until the letters have been filled in.   (Fig. 72).

A small speedball or ball-point pen may be used to fill in large or bold letters. It's faster than using a pointed pen and will keep the letters blacker than those filled in with a brush. Ink that has been brushed onto the drawing paper will often show an uneven tone after the paper has been cleaned with an eraser. This will not affect the reproduction, but does detract from the appearance of the caption when it is shown to the art buyer.

When the letters have been filled in, a fine-pointed pen should be used to sharpen any soft corners on the rigid strokes. Softened corners will damage the crisp appearance of these Gothic forms.

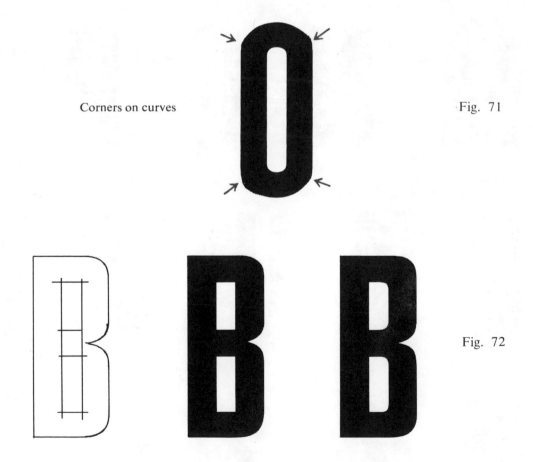

Corners on curves   ·Fig. 71

Fig. 72

Here's how a combination of Steel and Nylon makes this—the safest tire your money can buy

REVOLUTIONARY GASOLINE

$25,000 CASH

PROPORTION AND SPACING

The flat-sided Gothic capital alphabet contains eleven letters which are always identical in width. These are the B, C, D, G, H, O, P, Q, R, S, and U. When the bottom of the J arcs upward to end with a horizontal plane, this letter also should be drawn to the width of this group. These letters must be measured carefully to insure their relationship, as any difference will be quite obvious.

The E, F, L, T, and Z are drawn narrower than the above listed letters of identical width and can be condensed more than their standard relative proportion to the alphabet, when they appear in a tightly spaced line, in order to reduce the admitted white space. They must not, however, be crippled by too much condensing. A condensed line will almost inevitably produce some imbalance of white space, which must be accepted rather than narrowing the letters beyond the point of quick recognition. The letter L followed by an A, on a tightly spaced line is a typical example of an unavoidable hole in the line.   (Fig. 73).

The letters A, K, M, N, V, W, X, and Y are all wider than the letters of identical width; the M and W being the widest letters in the alphabet. The relative proportion of these wider letters should be gauged by eye. One should examine the admitted white spaces within these letters and try to judge their relationship to the white spaces within the narrower forms.

The letters of identical width are helpful in establishing the general letter relationships in any particular line.

The first run-throughs of a caption may be executed with a flat sketching pencil, chiseled to the approximate width of the stems or may be built up with a pointed 2B pencil over a light single-stroke indication. (Fig. 74). No measuring should be done on these preliminary tissues, but the *approximate* letter proportions and general spacing must be considered. When the required width of the caption has been reached, dividers should be used to determine the *average* width of all of the letters which must be identical in width, listed above, which appear in the caption. When the average width has been established, these letters must be measured as the second tissue progresses. If there are no major variations in the proportions of the wider and narrower letters, the second tissue should come reasonably close to the required width of the line.

Fig. 73

Fig. 74

During this development, the spacing of the letters must also be considered. There are several combinations of the balance between the weight of the stems, the white space within vertical letters, and the white space allowed between the letters. In a closely spaced line, the best readability is produced by making the width of the stems the widest measurement, the distance between letters slightly less in width, with the enclosed white spaces within the vertical letters being the narrowest measurement. (Fig. 75).

EVERY SMOKER WHO INHALES

Fig. 75

Other combinations of weights versus white space may not necessarily harm the legibility of a caption. One will find many captions in which the distance between the letters is the same as the white space within the letters. This combination can also be read quickly, but captions in which the enclosed white space is wider than the distance between letters rarely work out well, as the closeness of the vertical strokes will tend to produce a spotty caption. Only when very light-face letters are used should the white spaces be made wider than the letter strokes.

The combination to shun at all times, is the one in which the width of the stems, the enclosed white spaces, and the distance between characters are identical. This will produce a vibrating line that looks like a picket fence!

I have learned, from my experience as a teacher, that the rules which control the color adjustment in the Gothic forms are more readily assimilated when the study is begun with the more rigid flat-sided forms. Once the student has learned to use his ruling pen properly, the letters can be rendered more quickly than the rounded Gothic forms. The simplicity of their design will make the corrective color adjustments more obvious to the beginner.

The flat-sided letters offer a maximum of practice with the ruling pen. The pen should be held in a vertical position and pressed firmly against the straightedge. A clean pen, filled with reasonably fresh ink, requires no pressure against the paper to induce an even flow of ink—in fact, any downward pressure will dig the pen into the paper surface and cause an uneven weight in the line.

The ruling pen should be cleaned frequently during the ruling process and refilled with the feeder attached to the cork of the ink bottle.

A B C D E F

FLAT SIDED GOTHICS—LOWER CASE

The lower cases of the flat-sided forms are not as frequently lettered for major captions as are the capitals, but are always useful when combined with the capitals for words which require less accent, or as subcaptions.

The rules which govern the optical adjustment of weights on the capital letters, such as the diminishing weight on the diagonal lines, the thinning of curved and horizontal strokes, etc., apply to the lower cases as well. As these rules are described in detail in the previous section, there is no need to restate them here.

The relationship of the weight of the strokes to the white spaces within and between the letters should also be followed. The only exception to this balance of letter weights versus white space comes when these forms are lettered in lightface. Here, it becomes necessary to allow more white space within the letters than the width of the letter strokes in order to avoid condensing the letters to the point of illegibility. This situation automatically calls for wider spacing between the letters. If the vertical sides of the light-faces are placed too close together, the caption will tend to vibrate, due to the uneven distribution of color. (Fig. 76).

coloring

Fig. 76

The lower cases present a problem not found in the rendering of the capital forms—that of holding a balanced arc from the rigid stems into the lobes, or following stems. Note that on the type, these curves are more angular than the arc shown on the lettered forms. The latter curve does not dip as deeply into the rigid stem, and curves downward more quickly into the lobe or stem. The inside of the arc should be held to as near a symmetrical oval shape as possible. It should be remembered, however, that the need for optical weight adjustment still calls for a slight thinning of the stroke, as the curve is rounded. (Fig. 77).

Fig. 77

The lettered examples of lower cases shown on Plate 35 include acceptable variations in the design of the a, an alternate choice of a simplified g, and also for the t, which may be drawn as a straight line or curved forward at the bottom.

It should be noted that the a, b, c, d, e, h, n, o, p, q, s, and simplified g are all identical in width.

a b c d e f g
h i j k l m n
o p q r s t u
v w x y z

Plate 35

Alternate Gothic No. 1 type
lower case

184

a b c d e f g
h i j k l m n
o p q r s t u
v w x y z

Plate 36

Hand-lettered flat-sided
Gothic lower case

185

ROUNDED GOTHICS

Among the numerous Gothic type faces available today, the Futura alphabets continue to lead the field in popular usage. The weights are moderately adjusted to hold an optical evenness of tone and, with minor exceptions, the letter proportions are well related. Although some of the more recent cuttings of new Gothic forms have considerable merit, the Futuras should continue to hold a prominent place in the typographic field, and are a logical choice for a study of the rounded Gothic letters.

One might ask, in view of the fine qualities of the type, why they are so often hand lettered. Once again, the major reason is the fact that the lettering man can avail himself of the freedoms offered in drawing the letters, as against the restrictions that control mechanical type forms. While following the general design of the type letters, he can make any adjustments necessary to satisfy the requirements of the layout. The letters can be drawn in intermediate weights not available in type, expanded or condensed to fit into a given area, and the spacing can be improved. The letters are often inked in entirely freehand to give the caption a more casual effect than can be obtained through the use of type. The caption may also be designed with bounced letters to fulfill the requirements of a particular layout.

The same adjustments needed to produce the optical similarity of weights, described in the section on flat-sided Gothics, apply to the rendering of the Futura letters. These rules should be rechecked before a preliminary tissue is begun. However, it should be noted that rules which govern spacing, and the relationship of the inner white spaces to the weight of the line, do *not* apply to the Futura letters. Because these alphabets contain rounded shapes, the rules for spacing given on page 11 should be followed. The relationship of white space to weight of line is governed only by the degree to which letters have been expanded or condensed.

Examples of type and lettered capitals are shown on plates 36 and 37.

The color adjustments described in the preceding section have been made, to some degree, on the type forms but have been carried further on the hand lettering. The top or base of letters which contain diagonal lines has been drawn wider than the type design. The diminishing strokes in the A, K, M, N, V, W, X, and Y have been more consistently used on the lettered forms.

Only you can
PREVENT FOREST FIRES!

This Christmas
there's a Kodak outfit that's
just right for everyone

This "*Ounce of Prevention*"
Can Save Your Life!

A B C D E

F G H I J K

L M N O P

Q R S T U

Plate 37
Futura type—capitals

V W X Y Z

188

A B C D E

F G H I J K

L M N O P

Q R S T U

Plate 38
Hand-lettered Futura capitals

V W X Y Z

189

1 Note that the angled ending of the curves on the G, J, and S has been changed to the vertical endings used on the C. The outer corners of these vertical planes must be kept close to the horizontal guidelines to prevent distortion of the curves. The completely circular shape of the type G has been altered by the use of a vertical stroke drawn below the crossbar. These changes are almost invariably made on the boldface lettered forms, but are often followed on the lighter faces, as well.

2 The lobes of the B are kept in closer relationship in the lettered forms, but the lower lobe is still drawn a bit wider.

3 The M is usually lettered with vertical sides—an obvious aid to spacing.

4 The N is drawn narrower than the type form, holding the same width as the H and U.

5 The O and Q are generally drawn in an oval shape, instead of the circular type forms, except when all the letters are expanded. In this case, the O can go beyond the circular shape into a horizontal oval.

6 The diagonals on the lettered Y meet the stem at a lower point as an aid to better spacing.

7 The points of the type Z have been chopped into vertical planes and the letter is narrowed to reduce the admitted white space.

On the lower cases, note that the lobes of the lettered a, b, d, g, p, and q, and the curved strokes on the h, m, n, and u on Plate 39 are not dipped deeply into the vertical stems, as has been done on the type on Plate 38. The type forms were constructed this way in order to reduce a possible ink "bleed" at the merging point, when the type is used in small sizes or printed on soft paper stock. As the Futura forms are rarely lettered for small-size reproduction, the necessity of this quick thinning of the curves as they join the stems is eliminated. However, the arcs of the curves are still drawn a fraction thinner at the top and bottom, for optical correction.

On both type and lettered forms, the white spaces enclosed within the lobes of these letters are best held to a completely circular or oval form, depending upon their proportion. The arc of the white space must curve *into* the weight of the vertical stem. If this is not done, it will cause an optical weighting of the stem at this point. Some Gothic forms hold the flat plane of the stems on the inside of these letters but, in my opinion, the design of the Futura curves present a more pleasant connection of curves to the rigid strokes.

Note that the u has been drawn in the more generally used lower-case form in place of the small capital form used in the type alphabet.

The j also has been lettered with a swinging curve at the bottom, for quick recognition.

The angled ending of the curves on the type e, s, and j has been changed to the vertical plane ending of the c. The outer points of these vertical planes must be kept close to the horizontal guideline. If the corners are continued beyond this point, the top and bottom arcs will be distorted. The descender of the g may follow this design, in place of the horizontal ending of the arc.

The v, w, x, and y have been narrowed, and the diagonals diminished more in weight on the inside, as they travel toward the point of joining.

The points of the type z have been replaced by vertical planes and the letter has been narrowed.

190

A B C D E

F G H I J K

L M N O P

Q R S T U

V W X Y Z

Hand-lettered Futura capitals

a b c d e f
g h i j k l
m n o p q
r s t u v
w x y z

Plate 39
Futura type—lower case

a b c d e f

g h i j k l

m n o p q

r s t u v

w x y z

Plate 40
Hand-lettered Futura lower case

193

SPRYCRUST

Simple but Sensational!

Colgate Dental Cream

MOBILGAS

programs available 1956

UNION

7600

THE FINEST

PLEASE

A million dollars
a day into

HOW NOT TO DO IT

Shown below are examples of the most frequently recurring errors made by students when working on this alphabet.

The horizontal plane at the joining of the vertical and diagonal lines was not widened, resulting in a large admission of white space from the top and too little from below.

The vertical sides of this S are too short, caused by the too rapid descent of the center stroke.

Here, the crossbars were thinned too much producing the effect of a two-weight letter.

The diagonals diminish far too obviously which is just as bad as no adjustment at all.

The center crossbar has been placed too high, throwing the distribution of white space off balance and producing too long a tail on this R.

Not enough white space was dipped into the meeting of the two lobes.

The plane formed by the joining of the two diagonals was drawn much too wide which allowed the enclosed white space to almost cut the letter in half.

The diagonals of the Y have met the vertical stroke at too low a point producing a bottom-heavy letter.

The inner diagonals of the W were narrowed far more than was needed for optical correction.

The curves on the e were overly thinned which also makes the letter appear to be in the two-weight classification.

Here, no attempt was made to draw the balanced arc from the stem to the lobe.

The short stroke of the r has been allowed to angle sharply uphill instead of rolling from the stem.

So good to your TASTE

Fly the vibration-free
VISCOUNT to Nassau

Example of art director's lettering indication

197

LETTERING AND TYPE INDICATION

It is not by coincidence that the foremost art directors in the advertising field are generally able letterers. All good layout men know that the headline is one of the most important elements in an advertisement, serving to attract and hold the reader's attention. The art director who knows lettering can stimulate and inspire the lettering artist. I know from long experience that a lettering man always finds it easier to do a better job for art directors who know what they want in a caption and are able to indicate it understandably on a layout.

The layout student will find it much easier to indicate lettering after he has had considerable practice in inking finished captions. By first learning to draw the letters carefully, and thereby adding to his knowledge of the actual forms, he will be able to indicate them on layouts rapidly without having to resort to copy. When he begins to employ unusual styles and arrangements, the training in basic letter forms also will prove beneficial, in helping him to avoid illogical and hard-to-read captions.

Lettering on layouts must present a recognizable indication of the styles of lettering and type to be used in the advertisement. The proportions and spacing of the letters should be reasonably considered, so that the lettering specialist will be able to letter the finished captions without having to make major changes in height and weight. When a layout man fakes the proportion by jamming or extending letters in order to fill an allotted space, he may be creating a problem that will be difficult to solve when the advertisement goes into finished production. Very often the completed caption will differ considerably from the general effect of the indicated caption.

A beginner in layout work usually starts in the "bull-pen" of an advertising agency or as an assistant to an art director. From a lettering standpoint, he must be able to interpret the art director's ideas for the caption and to render them with reasonable speed— sometimes with unreasonable speed! The ability to indicate lettering and body text quickly is an asset in the advertising business, where the meeting of deadlines is essential. The larger advertising agencies can afford to nurse a promising beginner along, but in small agencies and art services, with a limited personnel and low budgets, the beginner is expected to cover his overhead costs, at least.

I don't mean that the captions, subcaptions, and body text need always be dashed off with frantic haste. As mentioned, they must be readable and workable. They should also be checked carefully for correct spelling, because misspelled words seem, strangely enough, to perturb the copywriters. What *must* be avoided is the common tendency among beginners to overpolish the comprehensive lettering. The beginner has the natural desire to display his ability and will often spend too much time in perfecting the individual letters. If he is unfamiliar with the letter forms, his unsureness will also cause a slow and painstaking rendering.

A highly important point to keep in mind is that the lettering indication must conform in its degree of finish to the other elements in the advertisement. If the illustrations are roughly sketched, the lettering must be roughly, though readably indicated. On carefully worked out layouts, the lettering must be in keeping with the general quality of the art work on the layout. At no time, however, should captions and subcaptions be lettered in such polished form that they give the impression of being finished lettering. This will definitely make the rest of the art work appear to be drawn roughly and carelessly.

Layout men know in advance whether a layout is intended for interoffice conferences or is to be presented to the client in more comprehensive form. The layouts made for interoffice discussion and planning are rarely worked up beyond the rough stage, because they are seen only by men whose training enables them to visualize the completed advertisement. The client usually prefers to see a more comprehensive presentation. The layout man or renderer should be able to produce a layout in varying degrees of development.

Although most layouts are sent to art services for the production of the presentation layout, the art director is always in a better position if he can execute a layout in both rough and comprehensive form.

PENCIL INDICATION

Captions indicated in pencil on layouts are done by two methods—the build up or stroke-out.

Some art directors prefer to build up all captions with a graphite or carbon pencil, while others use a chiseled-edge pencil to stroke out all the forms that can be produced with this tool. The chiseled pencil will produce a caption quickly, but built-up letters can also be done with satisfactory speed, after sufficient experience. The choice of these methods is just a matter of personal preference.

Practice on pencil indications should be done on tracing tissue or bond paper, as these papers are most often used for professional rough layouts.

Most formal or semiformal letters can be indicated with a chiseled pencil, after the caption has been single-stroked out lightly with a pointed pencil to establish its width and placement. Of course, the letters which were not developed from flat instrument renderings, can not be accurately indicated using this method. The way to get the optical effect of these letters is described in this section.

The pencil should be soft enough to stroke out a dark tone. At best, the grayness of the graphite can not match the solid black of the printed letters on the reproduced advertisement. It is difficult to judge the over-all balance of tone in a layout if the lettering indications are too light in value. A most important point to remember is that the letters must not vary greatly in tone. Uneven color is more damaging than carelessly indicated letters. When the other elements of the layout are in dark values, carbon or charcoal pencils should be used instead of graphite. As a time saver, when there is a lot of copy to be indicated, it is advisable to chisel several pencils to the desired width.

Letters done with a chiseled pencil may be stroked out freehand or held under more control by the use of a T-square and triangle for drawing the rigid strokes. I believe that the beginner should expose himself first to the greater discipline imposed by the use of straightedges. This approach is likely to be slow at the start, because it becomes necessary to free-stroke the curves more concisely to match the crisp, rigid strokes. However, if one starts out drawing the letters carefully, he will find that speed develops with practice and that his subsequent freehand renderings, done with even greater speed, will still hold a professional appearance. In other words, it's easier to loosen up one's renderings after a meticulous start, than it is to tighten up when the initial practice has been sloppy.

It must be understood, however, that perfection is never required in pencil indications. Many discrepancies can be overlooked if the *general* effect is sound.

All captions have an allotted space in an advertisement. The style, size, and arrangement are just one part of the over-all pattern of a layout. The caption might be lined up with the body text or with another element in the layout; used as a counterbalance, etc. Therefore, one of the first things a beginner must learn is to hold the caption to its given area in the layout, once its placement has been established. When a student begins to practice on pencil indications, he must impose restrictions upon himself from the start. The ability to indicate letters and to reach a specified width of line should be learned simultaneously.

The initial practice should be done on sheets of tissue or bond paper taped onto the drawing board cover. Horizontal guidelines must be lightly drawn to control the height of the letters. The copy of the caption should be *lightly* indicated with a single stroke of a pointed pencil. If this tentative indication is drawn in dark, it will show too obviously at points where the completed pencil caption has failed to cover some of the lines. While practicing, the light single-stroke indication should be considered as the specified width to be reached with the flat pencil stroke-out.

These restrictions will not be easy at the start. Most beginners will fall under or over the width many times and only a great amount of practice will solve the problem. Only by practice can one learn to judge the proportion and weight of letters while penciling them in single-stroke form.

The flat-sided Gothic Capitals offer the simplest letters on which to start this practice, as they contain a maximum number of rigid strokes. They should be tried at about an inch high, which will call for the use of a sketching pencil, narrowed to the desired width. The letters can be kept quite dark if a 4B is used for these large sizes. Even with the 4B, it is often necessary to run the pencil back and forth along the straightedge two or three times to produce a sufficiently dark tone.

After the caption has been lightly indicated, the vertical strokes should be drawn in first. The triangle must be held firmly against the T-square to prevent slipping. At this early stage of practice, it is best to stop when a letter with diagonal sides is reached and stroke them in, using the triangle for a straightedge, before continuing with the verticals. With more experience, one can learn to leave the space for these letters and put them in after completing the verticals.

When all the vertical and diagonal lines are drawn, the T-square is used for the horizontal strokes. Beginners often make the error of drawing the horizontal strokes too wide. It is better for the general spacing to keep them narrower than normal width, until one has learned to gauge the average proportion of these letters.

The curves must be stroked in freehand. This is the toughest part for most beginners and can be quite discouraging at the start. The flat of the pencil should be placed on the end of the vertical line and drawn in a curve as far as it will go without diminishing the weight of the stroke. The pencil is then lifted and placed against the edge of the short curve and the process repeated. Par for the course should be three strokes to complete the arc, but a student may find that he has to take more and shorter strokes at first. These curves need not be perfect, by any means. As long as they form a passable curve and are not drawn too far above or below the guidelines, the general effect will have been accomplished. Uneven joinings to the vertical strokes can be ignored.

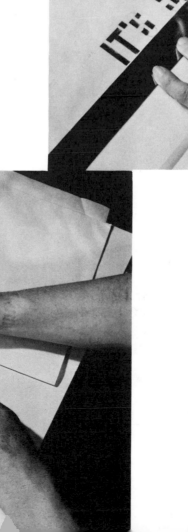

The capitals should be practiced in several weights and proportions
before starting the lower cases.

OUTSTANDING NEWS DISCOVERY

OUTSTANDING NEWS DISCOVERY

OUTSTANDING NEWS DISCOVERY

The lower cases should be tried at about one half the size of the capitals.
A narrowed sketching pencil may be used for the bolder faces and a
chiseled thick-lead drawing pencil for the lighter forms.

it makes fun out of driving...

it makes fun out of driving...

The rounded Gothics are the most difficult letters to indicate with a flat pencil. I have found that the average student can round the curves easier by drawing the center arc of each curve first, and then adding the strokes which join them or connect them to the stems. These letters should be practiced in the light faces only, at the start, because they are easier to master than the bolder forms.

a new delicious flavor

a new delicious flavor

SOMETHING NEW IN DETERGENTS

SOMETHING NEW IN DETERGENTS

SOMETHING NEW IN DETERGENTS

205

In stroking out the Bodoni letters, one must recognize the fact that the flat pencil will produce a constantly widening line as it rounds a curve, whereas the Bodoni characters contain curved hairlines of single weight. The natural action of the pencil can be overcome by using a minimum of pressure on the hairline strokes and then bearing down hard on the weighted strokes. The pencil still will produce the widening hairline curve, but the grayness of the stroke opposed to the dark tone of the weighted strokes will give the optical effect of the letters having very light, single-weight hairlines.

In order to keep the curved weights symmetrically balanced, the pencil edge should be held horizontally, rather than on the angle used to execute letters of the "humanistic" group. Almost inevitably, some off-balance curves will show up in the Bodoni stroke-outs, but if they are held to a minimum, the general effect of Bodoni letters will be produced.

A pointed pencil or the corner of the chiseled pencil should be used to put in the flat serifs.

NEW HAND LOTION

NEW HAND LOTION

charged with full power

charged with full power

There are many alphabets in which the lighter strokes are only slightly thinner than the weighted strokes. The Franklin Gothics are typical of this group. Other forms, such as Century, hold a fairly strong, lighter stroke, which must not be indicated as a hairline. It is advisable to chisel one pencil to the width of the heavy strokes and another for the lighter strokes to insure the proper relationship of the weights. On alphabets which contain bracketed serifs, this may be added with a pointed pencil after the stroke-out is completed, if time allows. On rough tissues, it's rarely necessary to take the time to add this final bit of polish.

LEADER IN THE LOW PRICE FIELD

LEADER IN THE LOW PRICE FIELD

LEADER IN THE LOW PRICE FIELD

The Formal Scripts are another style that is not a "natural" for flat-pencil indication. The pencil will not produce the swelling stroke which results from the use of a flexible pen. It will, however, place the below-center distribution of weight on the stroke in its correct position. As on the Bodoni, one must work for the general effect only, keeping the hairlines a very light-gray tone and bearing down on the weighted strokes.

For Glamorous hair that holds all day...

set your wave and hold your wave with

Formal Scripts should always be indicated freehand, drawn over a light, pointed-pencil write-out. Care must be taken to keep the letters on a fairly consistent diagonal.

The free-style scripts must also be worked up over a light pencil write-out.

Oh what a beautiful morning

Oh what a beautiful morning

This tentative write-out assumes more importance as it must be developed into the skeleton of the actual letters. In the indication of Formal Scripts, the light pencil write-out is used largely as a control for the width of the line, but the bounce and variations of the free-style scripts must be planned from the beginning. As described in the section on free-style scripts, the pattern of the line formed by the bounce and by the occasional use of boomed-up letters, must always be carefully considered. After the tentative write-out has been made, it should be gone over more carefully with a pointed pencil, firmly drawing in the actual skeleton of the letters. If the pattern of the bounce has produced a balanced line, the weights can then be added to the single-weight strokes to complete the caption.

Brush letters and brush scripts can only be simulated on pencil tissue roughs. A beginner will be better able to produce an acceptable brush effect with a pencil after he has learned to do these letters with his brush.

When he has observed the natural results of spontaneous brush writing, he can produce the general effect with a pencil. These letters are usually indicated in fairly rough form on pencil layouts, as any attempt to pin down the letters tends to make them look labored. A quick effect can be obtained by single or double stroking with a soft, blunt pencil—the number of strokes depending upon the weight of the letters. The layout man always tries to indicate these letters with a minimum number of strokes.

An entirely new gasoline

An entirely new gasoline

When the over-all tone of the layout calls for a dark value in the caption, the use of blunted carbon or charcoal pencils will be helpful. While making the tentative pencil stroke-out, one should roughly plot the approximate bounce and placement of the letters. These can be adjusted as the line is put in, but it is easier when one has a general arrangement to follow. The degree to which the brush scripts and brush letters are developed depends largely on how concisely the other elements in the layout have been drawn.

The art directors' pencil indications displayed in this section show the varying degrees of tangibility found on professional layouts. In some cases, the finished lettering worked from these indications, is shown.

The practice on the large sized Caslon letters suggested on pages 46-7, should make their execution in smaller sizes comparatively simple. The natural action of a flat pencil, held at a slight angle, will produce recognizable Caslon forms. There are many alphabets which contain basic strokes closely related to Caslons. These can be indicated by following the minor variations of design, possible changes in the relationship of thick to thin strokes, and changes in the shape of the serifs.

After considerable time has been spent on the flat pencil stroke-outs, using straightedges, the same styles should be practiced freehand, with a conscious attempt at speeding up the rendering time.

As mentioned earlier, all styles of lettering are often entirely built up with a pointed pencil. When practicing this method, one must remember that only a general effect is necessary. The professional work shown in this section is offered as examples of the various degrees of caption development to be found in the field.

It should be understood that many hours of practice must be put in on each style of lettering described here, before any degree of proficiency can be expected. These exercises are rarely easy at the start, but the hard work will pay off when a student applies his lettering indications on actual layouts.

210

Have <u>you</u>
had your
NUTRILITE
today?

Have <u>you</u>
had your
NUTRILITE
today?

212

BIG NEW VALUES!

TWA's
NEW STAR-WING
SUPER CONSTELLATIONS CAN FLY
NON-STOP
LOS ANGELES
TO LONDON

New way to make Cheese Sauce
in just 3 minutes!

Want
to
reduce?

Art director's indication

Finished lettering

Want
to
reduce?

214

8 garden-fresh vegetables
give you the lively flavor and goodness of V-8

You'll find
a dozen uses for
the nourishing
vegetable juices
in V-8

No __single__ juice can match
its lively flavor

Example of art director's lettering indication

Life Insurance
Companies show faith in Los Angeles...

Art director's indication

Finished lettering

Life Insurance
Companies show faith in Los Angeles...

Next year, take the vacation you really want

216

Never a Lump

Special Offer $**1**10 *this week only.... Regular price* 1.35

Carnation is the Secret of Failure-Proof Gravy

INK INDICATION

Ink or lampblack indications are usually used only on presentation layouts, which are to be shown to the client. These more careful renderings are done in the advertising agency's art department or sent to an art service, where the art director's rough layout is developed into presentation form.

Presentation lettering in ink calls for more preparation than needed for pencil indications. The caption may be roughly developed on tracing tissue and traced through onto the paper, or lightly indicated in actual letter forms directly onto the paper. In each case, the pencil indications must give assurance that the caption will fit into the planned area.

Either a pen or brush may be used for rendering ink comprehensives. The pen will produce a crisper effect, when necessary, but many layout men and renderers prefer the brush because it develops the letters more quickly.

On all ink comprehensives, one should learn to make additional adjustments with the pen or brush while inking. It must be remembered that minor discrepancies are allowable in comprehensives and that time is an important factor. One must avoid the natural tendency to produce a small finished caption which will not harmonize with the other elements in the layout. If the caption is held to the *general* characteristics of a letter and the weights kept reasonably alike, the indication will fulfill the requirements.

It is advisable when using a pen to choose one large enough to draw the hairlines with no building up. On heavy-serif letters, the use of a larger pen is equally logical. Too small a pen will cause a niggly stroke which can use up a lot of time.

When lettering on bond paper or toothy stock, the pen

should be held lightly with very little pressure applied. The smaller letters need not be inked in solidly, but too much white paper should not be allowed to show through the letters as this will appear to be a studied technique. This also applies to the inking of hairlines. When letters contain thin hairlines, the pen should barely touch the paper in order to keep the lines as light as necessary. This light touch often results in broken or detached hairlines, which adds to the spontaneous quality of the execution. However, it is best to avoid the deliberate breaking of these lines as they, too, will appear to be studied.

The comprehensive rendering of brush scripts and brush letters can rarely be done by a direct write-out with the brush. It is safer to plan the caption on tissue until the lettering is contained within the allotted area and traced onto the paper. The letters should then be built up with a brush, with an attempt made to imitate the spontaneous strokes of an actual brush-out.

If one has trouble in holding the true vertical or diagonal of the formal letters, guidelines should be traced *through* the tissue. Do not draw these guidelines on the paper as they will be harder to erase. Heavy erasure will often pick up the ink lettering from bond papers or toothy illustration boards. Retouching with white paint should be held to a minimum on comprehensive lettering. White paint should be used to clean up only the major slips in draftsmanship and tone, allowing all other raggedness to remain.

The ink indications, reproduced in actual size, are shown here in varying degrees of comprehensive rendering. One is rarely required to indicate lettering more carefully than the examples shown.

There's a wonderful difference in Mobilgas Special*

Art director's indication

220

There's a wonderful difference in Mobilgas Special*

Finished lettering

They'll feel better
if you go on a TWA
Super Constellation
and you will too!

YOU'LL GET THERE FASTER...YOU'LL TRAVEL IN LUXURY...
AND YOU'LL FLY ON AMERICA'S SAFEST TRANSCONTINENTAL AIRLINE

---

4 TIMES AS MANY ORDERED AS
NEAREST U.S. TYPE
TWICE AS MANY AS FOREIGN JET TYPE

The swing in air travel is to

Super Constellation
STYLE

Stockholder's Meeting

Art director's indication

Stockholders' Meeting

Finished lettering

6 New and Better Recipes
Made Possible by Carnation's
Special Blending Qualities
and Double Richness

No other form of milk will do

TYPE INDICATION

There are several methods of indicating the type for the body text in a layout. The type indications must conform to the degree of finish of the other elements in a layout, as well as the indicated lettering.

Shown here are various forms of indication. The number 1 through 6 group is generally used on tissue layouts, although some art directors prefer the use of the pencil on bond and illustration board comprehensives.

The thin lines should be drawn with a soft pencil. If there is much copy to be indicated, keep several pencils sharpened to avoid thickening of the lines as the pencil point becomes blunt.

1 Thick lines are ruled with a chiseled pencil. These lines should be held to a medium gray tone. These wide lines are sometimes used to indicate a subcaption, with the line broken into word lengths.

2 Lines are ruled with a chiseled pencil, using short strokes to produce variation of tone in each line.

3 Single lines are ruled closer together than an actual typeset to approximate the mass tone of the type.

4 Double lines are ruled to the approximate point size of the type to be used.

5 Double lines are ruled with a pointed pencil using short strokes to produce variation of tone on each line.

6 Looped lines, broken into word length, are drawn between lightly indicated guidelines.

1

2

3

4

5

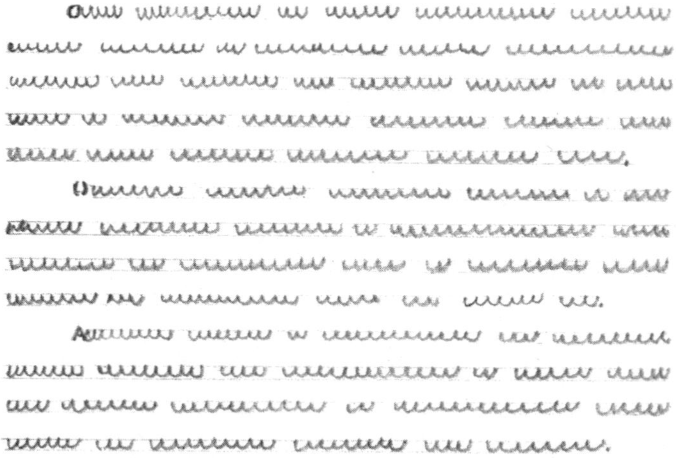

6

On comprehensive layouts done on heavy bond, drawing paper, or illustration board, the thin ruled lines are usually put down with a ruling pen, using either ink or dark gray paint. If gray paint is used, it should be mixed to a flowing consistency and fed to the ruling pen with a brush. The pen should be tested on a sheet of paper similar to the paper actually being worked on to make sure that the line is the right thickness and that the paint will flow evenly.

The looped lines and the simulated individual letters are drawn with a pointed pen. The general effect of type can be achieved by using a majority of vertical lines relieved by an occasional curved shape. When the text is to be set in lower case, as is most often done, some ascenders and descenders should be indicated.

The gray paint should be fed to the pointed pen with a brush and the surplus shaken off. The flow of the paint should be tested on a similar sheet of paper before working on the layout. As the paint tends to dry quickly on a pointed pen, the pen point must be washed regularly during any lengthy indication. A more realistic effect will be produced by changing the length of each paragraph and varying the width of word indications.